# I WAS WINSTON CHURCHILL'S
## PRIVATE SECRETARY

# I WAS
# WINSTON
# CHURCHILL'S
# PRIVATE
# SECRETARY

by

## PHYLLIS MOIR

WILFRED FUNK, INC.
PUBLISHERS        NEW YORK

COPYRIGHT, 1941, BY WILFRED FUNK, INC.

First printing April, 1941
Second printing April, 1941
Third Printing May, 1941

PRINTED IN THE UNITED STATES OF AMERICA
BY THE CORNWALL PRESS, INC., CORNWALL, N. Y.

*With Affection*

*to*

HENRY GODDARD LEACH

*who introduced me to*
*Winston Churchill*

# INTRODUCTION

Miss Phyllis Moir's book is charming, so interesting and such easy reading that I found to my regret that I was already more than half way through when I thought that I had only just commenced to read it.

The references to Winston Churchill brought back memories of schools where we were together, and many of which I had forgotten; but looking back I can realize that even then he had an extraordinary personality. At Harrow this was most noticeable. Out of some eight hundred boys there were probably very few who did not know of him, in spite of the fact that he was neither in his House eleven nor in the Upper school.

This was continued through life, as when during the Boer War the whole British Army in South Africa was acutely interested in his escape from the prison camp when he was a newspaper correspondent at the time.

It is always interesting to read of the foibles of

a very great man, for our lion-hearted Prime Minister has proved himself to be even more than a very great man; they make him so splendidly human. These traits so amusingly set forth will, if possible, endear him more than ever to the people of the United States.

Mr. Churchill is almost typical of the old Roman days when that nation was at its zenith. He has ability to turn from grave affairs of State to painting pictures, or even laying bricks.

As one reads these pages it comes home to one that perhaps Mr. Churchill's outstanding characteristic is that he is the strong man who can afford to break with tradition if he thinks that it is wise. And the people who disagreed with him have nearly always been people of a fixed state of mind.

At school as in later life his personality and brilliance attracted attention, even if these traits, except in times of great national emergencies, excluded him from the inner circle of the Regulars.

GOSFORD

*The Earl of Gosford*

Miss Phyllis Moir came to me with very high recommendations which have been completely justified. She is not only an excellent stenographer, but is a highly competent Private Secretary, able to write letters on her own judgment, and to keep accounts.

She is also an excellent traveller, and in every way competent, trustworthy and agreeable. I can most cordially recommend her to anyone having need of capable and confidential assistance of this kind.

*Winston S. Churchill*

A LETTER OF COMMENDATION FROM MR. CHURCHILL

# CONTENTS

*Chapter I*

# I CHOOSE MY COURSE

❖

I HAVE SPENT a large part of my life recording with pencil and paper the words and thoughts of men and women whom the world has generally considered famous. To many people this might seem a thankless way of living the one life one has to live. I frankly confess I have found it otherwise. There is much innocent excitement to be derived from association with figures in the public eye.

It struck me long ago that the next best thing to a leading role on the world stage is a discreetly strategic position in the wings, where you can enjoy the play, study the acting, and indulge in your little private laugh at the foibles of the actors without offending their susceptibilities.

I got my first job as a secretary at the age of

seventeen. Very soon I graduated to the more responsible realm of private secretaryship, and pursued that career with all its ramifications—business manager, companion, confidential adviser, and other duties—for nearly twenty years. On the whole I found the work absorbing and not devoid of adventure.

It is amusing, if one has a sense of humor and a certain natural detachment, to spend a few years working for this celebrity, a few years for another. You travel; you meet the people who are shaping the world you live in; you can contemplate at leisure the qualities that make for greatness and the weaknesses that go with them; you can learn a great deal about your fellow men and women. It is a comfortable, civilized, intelligent life.

Not long ago I forsook all these advantages for the trials and tribulations of publishing. I joined the staff of a national magazine, and plunged into the hectic existence of a managing editor at a time when three-quarters of one's job consisted in keeping a magazine alive. Why, you may well ask, did I do it? Because of Mr. Winston Churchill.

I must hasten to explain this.

[ 4 ]

Before working for Mr. Churchill I had been associated with a succession of prominent men and women—Lord Robert Cecil, Lord Derby, Sir Nevile Henderson, Mr. Arthur Balfour, who later became Lord Balfour, Mrs. O. H. P. Belmont, Miss Winifred Holt, Miss Lillian Gish, when she was at the height of her fabulous career, and a number of others. Most of them had left me with agreeable recollections, tinged in some cases with respect, in others with affection. But with Mr. Churchill it was quite different. The impact of his personality was so shattering that I felt, when I left his service, that this had been the private secretaryship to end all private secretaryships—so far as I was concerned.

Mr. Churchill, I was forced to conclude, was a true case of genius. The man had faced every side of life fairly and squarely and had mastered them all, a perfectly rounded man with a hundred horsepower brain and an insatiable zest for living. Working closely with Mr. Churchill was like watching a Duse or a Sarah Bernhardt every night from the wings. From now on I knew there could be little excitement or adventure in working for a lesser man.

Winston Churchill caught my imagination when I was still a schoolgirl in pigtails. Already he was a legendary figure—dashing, romantic, rebellious. The papers were full of him, his mad political somersaults, his marriage to "the most beautiful girl in England," his spectacular doings as Home Secretary.

I remember hearing my father once mutter to himself over his morning newspaper, "He'll get to the top, that young chap, if his cleverness doesn't ruin him. It's not good for a politician to be too brilliant."

But to the gawky schoolgirl sitting dreamily at the breakfast table in a very quiet, staid little English town brilliance was a glowing attribute. I was in those days, I must confess, a romantic worshiper of Winston Churchill, descendant of the famous Duke of Marlborough, who, we were told in our little red history books, had won the glorious victories of Blenheim, Ramillies, and Malplaquet in the time of Good Queen Anne. I didn't suspect then that this romantic Mr. Churchill would one day be summoning me from a nice warm bed in the early hours of the morning to dictate a letter to the Prime Minister of Australia or the Prince of an Indian border state. I never dreamt that in the years to come the dashing young ex-officer of the Hussars would be a rotund, middle aged gentleman, sitting up in bed in cream-colored pajamas, puffing at a strong-smelling cigar, as he fired a torrent of words at the head of his harassed private secretary—myself.

To Phyllis Moir of Miss Dolby's School for Young Ladies, Winston Churchill was a Walter Scott hero come to life. I was a rebellious, imaginative little girl who spent half her time daydreaming and the other half devouring historical novels. Scott, Dumas, and Charles Kingsley were my favorite authors. By the time I was twelve I alas knew *Kenilworth, Westward Ho!* and *The Three Musketeers* by heart. The tidy, unimaginative, humdrum pattern of English life in that safe and comparatively uneventful pre-war world seemed to me dreadfully unsatisfying. Most of the men in the public eye were staid, dignified, pompous old gentlemen, sadly disappointing to my youthful fancy. Whenever I could I would escape to my fiction world of adventure and excitement to snatch enchanted interludes in the spacious times of Queen Elizabeth and Henry VIII, to move breathlessly among brave men and beautiful ladies in the courts of Europe, and to forget in the glorious, chivalrous, dazzling past the monotonous routine prescribed for me by teachers and parents.

I grew to detest the compulsory school games and the unbearably long Sunday walks. The attitude of my fellow students, who accepted this life as a matter of course, seemed to me cowardly and infuriating. I decided that they were boring and commonplace; but this conclusion I prudently kept to myself.

One clear, frosty evening on my way home from school, laden with books for the evening's homework, I solemnly resolved to escape from it all as soon as I could. Then and there, with the dark wintry sky as my only witness, I dramatically vowed that somehow or other I would make life a shining, exciting adventure. I would travel to remote corners of the earth. I would meet great and interesting people, people who had dared to step out of the rut of a commonplace, conventional existence. Fired with this ambitious resolution, I applied myself with fanatical energy to my French and history lessons—in preparation, I told myself sagely—for the sort of life I was planning.

The World War, which brought an end to so many promising young lives, opened for me the door to desired opportunities. Its immediate effect on my life was to make school seem more unbearable than ever. During a visit to London I borrowed some hairpins, tucked my pigtails into a tight knot at the back of my head, and wearing what I hoped would pass for a "grown up" hat, I presented myself at the recruiting offices of the Women's Army Auxiliary Corps, which was then taking on volunteers for various types of service with the army. I walked into the majestic hall of Devonshire House almost paralyzed with apprehension, but with a clear idea in my mind as to what I wanted to do. Some time before this, at Waterloo station, I had seen some smartly uniformed women ambulance drivers setting off for France. They were the "First Aid Nursing Yeomanry" or "Fannies," as people used to call them. To become a "Fanny" at once seemed to me a passport to glamour and adventure.

When I came before the examining board of very dignified, severe-looking army officers, my beautiful dream was immediately shattered. The head of the Board took one look at me and with a benevolent twinkle in his eye informed me I was far too young. Seeing my disappointment, he patted me kindly on the shoulder and told me to go back to school and forget about it. I cried all the way back to the hotel.

For the time being I took his advice but soon gained my long-suffering mother's permission to take a secretarial course in London. Night and day I slaved at shorthand and typing. In the conquest of those agonizing hieroglyphics lay the key to my future. When I took a secretarial test at the Ministry of Munitions, where a distant cousin of mine, Sir Ernest Moir, held an important post, I passed with flying colors.

In the Hotel Metropole in London, then the headquarters of the Ministry of Munitions, I met Winston Churchill face to face for the first time. I was walking along one of the corridors, when a side door suddenly opened and a short, stocky figure charged out. For a second I stared at a round, pink face and a pair of prominent blue eyes. But the apparition had vanished round the corner before I had time to realize "So that is Mr. Churchill."

His personality dominated the Ministry, of which he was then in charge. In a few months he had performed a miracle of reorganization and the Ministry of Munitions was already a model for the other war departments. Winston Churchill's mere presence in the building seemed to set a faster tempo for every clerk and typist. Occasionally some report or memorandum would be brought to my desk to be typed for Mr. Churchill, invariably with the request that it had to be done in a tremendous hurry because "Mr. Churchill wants it right away." How familiar that phrase became in after years when I was his private secretary! At the time it merely struck me as rather odd that Mr. Churchill should always be in a hurry.

I continued to regard my job at the Ministry of Munitions as a step towards my real goal which was to go abroad. I didn't much care in what capacity. Since the women's services at the front were closed to me on account of my youth I decided to investigate other possibilities. The passive attitude toward life has never appealed to me and I have found, in return, that life responds generously to the individual who steers his own course. In this case, I didn't have far to seek or long to wait for the job I wanted.

Someone, I can't remember who, told me that the Foreign Office was looking for women secretaries to join the clerical staff of some of the European Embassies. The burden of work caused by the war had proved too heavy for the regular diplomatic staffs, and for the first time in the history of the British Empire women were to be allowed to work in the Chancelleries. I immediately hurried to the Foreign Office, armed with what seemed to me an imposing array of letters of recommendation. The Foreign Office also apparently found them imposing. I was immediately accepted. Two weeks later, clutching a new passport with a diplomatic visa, I stepped onto a Channel steamer at Southampton on my way to the British Embassy in Paris.

I was the first woman to be sent out by the Foreign Office to that huge, green-gray building set in a spacious courtyard on the Faubourg St. Honoré. It was a very different world from the noisy, informal, rough-and-tumble of the Ministry of Munitions. Here no one hurried. People spoke in discreetly hushed tones. Only very minor persons put in an appearance before 10:30 in the morning. "His Excellency" the Ambassador was assisted by a staff whose names read like a page from Burke's Peerage. I found it all very impressive.

In the huge general office known as the Chancery the diplomatic secretaries decoded messages of world-shattering importance. They slowly and laboriously typed their memoranda on long blue sheets of paper for transmission to the Foreign Office in the Embassy pouch, which went back and forth to London by King's Messenger.

There was only one filing clerk. He bore the dignified title of archivist, an extremely old and crochety individual who had lived in Paris for thirty years without learning a single word of French. He spent his days among his dusty archives, docketing the long blue Foreign Office dispatches in his copperplate handwriting and tying them up affectionately with red tape. He, more than anyone else on the staff, sternly disapproved of the introduction of women into the hitherto monastic atmosphere of the Embassy. Whenever, by some unlucky chance, he met me on the stairs, he would duck his head and pass me by without uttering a word. Never once did he unbend.

Sir Nevile Henderson, then plain Mr. Henderson, was Third Secretary of the Embassy at that time. Handsome and distinguished, with a ready sense of humor, he was one of the favorite bachelors of Paris. My first contact with him came only a few weeks after my arrival when he breezed into my office to ask if I would like to join the diplomatic staff of the Embassy in a round-robin appeal to the Foreign Office for an increase in our salaries. It had not taken me long to discover that my pay-check, which had seemed so generous in London, did not go far in wartime Paris with its high prices for food and rent. Refugees from the conquered areas were overrunning the pensions and hotels. Prices were skyrocketing. It would never have occurred to me to make any protest about it. I was much too proud of my new job to find any fault with it. But Mr. Henderson thought otherwise. His organized and energetic protest brought quick results. Everyone got a raise.

Paris at that time was an exciting place for a

girl just out of school and the Embassy was a thrilling place to work in. I was pleasantly reminded of it all by a letter received recently from Sir Nevile Henderson harking back to the last war. "I like to think that your experience at the Paris Embassy helped you build your career," he remarked, and no doubt it has.

The Embassy then was, or so it seemed to its youngest member, the center of the world. A constant stream of important messages for the French Government from the British Foreign Office poured in to our offices daily. Across the courtyard the Ambassador would be receiving high Allied officials, while the less august personages came in to the Chancery to confer with the Counsellor or other members of the diplomatic staff.

Day in and day out important memoranda and lengthy diplomatic letters in French and English were reeled off my typewriter and I soon became thoroughly familiar with the pompous, roundabout jargon of diplomatic correspondence.

On the staff we had two future Ambassadors, Sir Eric Phipps and Sir Nevile Henderson. Sir Nevile was Ambassador to Berlin when the Second

World War was declared and Sir Eric Phipps had been his predecessor in that office.

Of the visiting diplomats I liked best to work for Mr. Arthur Balfour and Lord Robert Cecil. Both of them were possessed of that extraordinary old-world sense of courtesy now so rare. They would rise politely whenever I entered the room in answer to a summons to take dictation, and always treated me as a guest rather than as a secretary.

Mr. Churchill, often in Paris on official business, was a frequent visitor to the Embassy. Whenever I caught a glimpse of him it was of a short, stocky figure with shoulders already beginning to stoop, smoking a cigar and in a desperate hurry to get somewhere.

By the Spring of 1918 the streets of Paris were filled with American officers and men attached to the various army headquarters. My hotel was invaded by American army doctors who had served with the British on the terrible Ypres salient and had been sent back to Paris for a rest. In spite of the fact that "Big Bertha" had started its long-range bombardment of the city life, for me at least, became a very gay affair. When the air-raid

[ 16 ]

sirens sounded all the occupants of the hotel would gather in the cellar, there to hold impromptu concerts and drink hot mulled wine generously supplied by the management.

English and American girls were few and far between in Paris in the war years and those of us who were there had the time of our lives. I was swamped with invitations to lunch and dinner, dancing and the theatre by Americans who hadn't had a chance to talk English to a woman for months.

It was my first introduction to American men and I liked them at once. I was especially taken by their style of dancing. It was that that really decided me to go to America as soon as the war was over. As a matter of fact there were no public dances in Paris during the war but the Red Cross gave frequent "hops" for English and American soldiers, and these were pretty hard work for the feminine contingent as there were generally about 20 girls to some 300 men, all of them determined not to miss a dance!

I remember attending a grand banquet given by the American officers at my hotel. It was quite an international affair. Round the table were the uniforms of most of the Allied armies, Rumanian, Italian, British, Polish and others. After dinner— it was an oppressively hot night—some of us went out for a breath of air. We were standing on the corner of the Champs Elysees hoping for a cool breeze when an earthshaking roar suddenly shook the windows of the houses behind us. We looked at one another in astonishment. There was another roar; and this time the noise continued like the rumble of distant thunder. We asked a passing French officer what it could be. He grinned happily, "It's the big Allied push," he said. "Only just beginning but we'll soon have them on the run now that the Americans are with us."

He proved to be a true prophet. The gloom of that year rapidly gave place to a frenzy of activity as the German army began to crumble before the Allied offensive. And the Embassy, in a very dignified way of course, began to reflect the changed spirit of the time. Every morning toward the end of October, long, gray cars would sweep into the courtyard bringing Foch, Pershing, Haig, and the other Allied commanders for lengthy conferences with French and British statesmen. Standing with my nose glued to the window of my office, I watched their arrival with a sense of mounting excitement.

One morning Sir Eric Drummond burst excitedly into my office carrying a two-page manuscript which, he said, had to be copied immediately for transmission to the Foreign Office by the King's Messenger who was waiting. It contained the terms of the Armistice! He stood beside me while I typed it and when it was handed to him he said solemnly, "This is the most important document that has ever gone out of this Embassy." I'm afraid I was far too young to have been suitably impressed. But there was something that even Sir Eric did not realize then. Those two typed pages have probably done more than any other single factor to determine the disastrous course of the last twenty years of Europe's history.

Just before this Lord Derby had been appointed Ambassador to Paris upon the death of Lord Bertie of Thame. His position was much the same as that of Lord Halifax today. The Paris Embassy was then, as the Washington Embassy is today, the key position on the diplomatic front. Sir Austen Chamberlain, General Smuts and Lord Milner had all been considered for the job but finally it was decided to ask Lord Derby to resign from the Cabinet as Secretary of State for War to take over this vital post.

Lord Derby made an instant hit with the French. True, he did not speak their language, but there was something so healthily John Bullish, so friendly, so reassuring about his manner that wherever he went he made just the right impression. I was occasionally summoned to take dictation from him and found him an easy man to work for, affable and informal. His outdoor appearance, somewhat like the caricaturist's idea of a robust country squire, made him seem amusingly out of place amid the ornate surroundings of the Embassy, its glittering chandeliers, the spindly gilt chairs, the marble-topped tables and polished rosewood cabinets.

After the Armistice King George and his two sons, the young, fair-haired Prince of Wales and his brother the Duke of York, came to spend a few days at the Embassy. There was very little work done in the offices while they were there. Every time a footfall was heard in the courtyard the female members of the staff—by this time there were six of us—would rush to the windows in the hope of catching a glimpse of the two young princes. One day I nearly had a head-on collision with them in the doorway of Houbigant's, the perfumer. They were laughing so heartily about something as they emerged from the shop that they failed to notice me about to enter. The Prince of Wales blushingly apologized for his carelessness and I, like every other girl in Paris, thought him the most attractive and charming young man I had ever seen.

After the King returned to England Lord Derby gave a grand reception for the Prince of Wales at the Embassy. It was a gala occasion since it really constituted the first formal appearance of the young Prince on the international scene.

During the Peace Conference the Hotel Majestic, which housed the enormous British delegation, became the social center of Paris. Every Saturday night we were all invited to a huge ball. These assemblies were the gayest and most glittering I have ever seen. The men, the most distinguished men in Europe, appeared in resplendent uniforms, their chests adorned with medals, orders and crosses; the women, the most beautiful women in Europe, shone in the glory of a fashion that sought to blot out the memory of four hideous years of war. The music was superb. The suppers were elaborate, a marvel of plenty after four lean years of rationing. And in a very dry vintage champagne we drank toasts to the new world made safe for democracy. It was the natural setting for a Churchill. I saw him time and again admiring a lovely gown or talking earnestly to Lloyd George, Arthur Balfour or Bonar Law, sipping his champagne with the keen enjoyment of a man who loves the best of everything.

Sir Ernest Moir, who was Lord Cowdray's partner in the Pearson Oil Company, often came to the Embassy on business. He was one of Lloyd George's technical assistants on the Peace Conference. To him I confided my longing to go to America and received in return a sympathetic promise that he would give me letters of introduction to his influential friends in the United States. Sir Ernest seemed quite American himself. He had spent a great many years in the United States and in Mexico. As a young engineer he had worked on the Hudson Tunnel. He was a kindly, bluff Scotchman and spoke admiringly of his former chief, Winston Churchill.

"It's a joy to work for him," I once heard him say. "There's a lot of the Yankee in Winston. He knows how to hustle and how to make others hustle too." Years later I had good cause to remember his words!

After the Peace Conference life in Paris quietened down considerably and I decided that then was the moment to move on. It so happened that my desire to visit America was very soon satisfied. After a short interlude at the British Embassy in Rome I met Miss Winifred Holt, head of the New York Association for the Blind in Europe, and I came to this country as her private secretary.

That first visit of mine was short-lived. In less than a year we returned to Europe on a relief mission to Poland, then ravaged by disease and starvation. For weeks, in that icy winter, we traveled from one refugee camp to another on the bleak Polish-Russian border, living amongst the dead and dying, giving what cheer and comfort we could to the handful of devoted doctors, nurses, and civilian volunteers who were struggling heroically to check the spread of the dread oriental typhus amongst the starved and frozen refugees.

After returning to the United States I met Miss

Lillian Gish, the movie star. When she signed her famous $8000-a-week contract with Metro-Goldwyn-Mayer she telegraphed me to join her in Santa Monica, California. I was with her during the years she made "La Boheme," "The Scarlet Letter," "Wind" and other famous pictures of the pre-talkie era.

Then came my job with Mr. Churchill.

Close contact with the great is generally disappointing. But not so with Churchill. My association with him has in general confirmed the picture I had cherished as a romantic schoolgirl, even though it has placed my picture of him in a more accurate and a more sober perspective. It also convinced me quickly that this was the man England might turn to should she ever find herself in serious danger. It doesn't take long to sense that Winston Churchill is one of those rare spirits born to lead other men.

*Chapter II*

# I MEET THE MAN

❖

A SUCCESSION OF FORTUNATE coincidences resulted in my becoming Mr. Churchill's private secretary.

I had just arrived in the East from Hollywood when I read in an evening paper that Mr. Churchill had the same day landed in America. The picture of Mr. Churchill, beaming genially at the cameramen and smoking a long cigar, stirred faintly exciting recollections of wartime days in the Ministry of Munitions and the Paris Embassy and of a short, stocky figure charging down corridors, sending memoranda to be typed "in a desperate hurry," always shaking up people's settled habits and speeding up the tempo of everything around him.

Since then I had followed his career with keen interest but I had not seen him for several years.

The last occasion, however, had been in its way memorable. I had sat directly behind him in the stalls of a London theatre the night he astonished Mayfair by taking time off from his duties as Chancellor of the Exchequer at the most critical moment of the General Strike to see a musical comedy. The English upper classes and all the Americans in London were convinced that this was the beginning of The Revolution and were naturally greatly reassured when they saw Mr. Churchill gaily enjoying the performance as though all were for the best in the best of all possible Englands.

As all this came back to me I remember thinking idly it would be quite an adventure to be Mr. Churchill's secretary. A few weeks later the "adventure" was almost thrown at my head.

As soon as Mr. Churchill landed in America he set about looking for a private secretary. He simply can't live without one. Mr. Vincent Sheean, who wished to study Churchill at close quarters, applied for the job but being an American was not eligible. Mr. Churchill was in close correspondence with the British Government and was therefore anxious to have a British-born person as his secretary. A good friend of mine, Mr. George Jean Nathan had recommended me to Dr. Henry Goddard Leach, editor of *Forum Magazine,* for a position on his staff. Dr. Leach had no vacancies at the time but had heard from a friend that Mr. Churchill was having some difficulty in finding the right person to work for him and suggested me for the job.

On a cold, snowy afternoon a few days after Christmas I knocked at the door of Apartment 39A in the Tower of the Waldorf-Astoria, the Churchill's apartment. A tall, lanky man with an angular cockney face opened the door. I discovered later that he was Sergeant—now Inspector—Thompson of Scotland Yard, Mr. Churchill's private "shadow."

"I have an appointment with Mr. Churchill," I said just a trifle nervously.

My friends agree that I am a very harmless-looking person but Sergeant Thompson eyed me suspiciously and gave me a professional once-over.

"Come in, Miss," he said, a little reluctantly I thought, having apparently satisfied himself that I was not a cunningly disguised Hindu terrorist. "I'll tell Mr. Churchill you're here."

He took me into a terribly crowded little room filled with trunks and packing-cases. Filing boxes, stationery supplies and piles of correspondence seemed to be heaped on every table and chair. A harassed looking woman was pounding furiously at a typewriter. She seemed too busy even to notice me. Sergeant Thompson disappeared. After about twenty minutes he returned.

"Mr. Churchill will see you now, Miss," he said in a marked cockney accent. "You'll find him pretty weak and tired," he went on chattily. "That accident * gave him a nasty jolt and he only came out of the hospital a few days ago."

Sergeant Thompson ushered me into a spacious drawing-room sumptuously furnished in the English style. The walls were adorned with brightly colored hunting prints. At first I thought the room was unoccupied. Then, buried in an enormous Queen Anne armchair by a blazing fire, I caught sight of a humpty-dumpty sort of figure reading a letter.

It was Winston Churchill.

At first he didn't seem to notice that I was there

---

* About a fortnight before Mr. Churchill had been hit and seriously injured by an automobile.

and I had time to take stock of my future employer. I had hit upon Mr. Churchill on what must have been one of the lowest ebbs of his life. The accident had left him in a state of complete physical exhaustion. A deep, livid gash in his forehead gave him the air of a sorely wounded warrior and the droop of his powerful shoulders betrayed a weariness which the jauntiness of his attire could not disguise.

He was wearing a brown pinstripe suit with a brown and white polka-dot bow tie to match; a white linen handkerchief stuck gaily out of his breast pocket and his feet were encased in black buttoned boots with odd looking cloth tops. He was smoking a huge cigar and a pile of ash had collected on the folds of his waistcoat. I was fascinated by his small, delicate, beautifully shaped hands—the hands of an artist.

At Mr. Churchill's elbow was a tray with a bottle of Scotch whiskey, a siphon of soda and a half-empty glass. On another and larger table at his side rested a blue leather dispatch box with a brass handle and the initials W.S.C. engraved on the lid in gold letters. Next to it was a neat pile of books and a bowl of pink roses. The windows of the apartment were wide open to the icy winter air. I glimpsed a glittering Christmas tree in a corner, the sharp red of poinsettia plants, and a profusion of flowers—lilacs and red carnations.

Eventually Mr. Churchill looked up and said, rather distantly, "I understand you are willing to accompany me on my peregrinations."

I can't remember what I replied because the next minute he waved the letter he was reading at me and remarked sternly, "You shouldn't have sent me the originals of these letters—your letters of recommendation. They're far too valuable. Why, they might have got lost."

I stood there feeling rather like a schoolgirl who has been reproved for misconduct by a formidable headmistress.

It was quite a shock to me to discover that the dashing young man I had admired years before had matured into such a terrifying personality. I am not by nature a timid person and after three years in Hollywood one is not easily impressed by anyone. But Churchill literally floored me. Never in my life have I felt so unimportant beside another human being.

Then quite abruptly his manner changed. "I

was particularly interested in this one from a relative of yours, Sir Ernest Moir," he said smiling. "He worked very closely with me in the war and I have a great respect for his judgment. I'm going to Nassau and will be back in a few weeks. Will you be ready to start work then?"

"Yes," I replied, and waited for further questions.

"Well, that's that," Mr. Churchill said, and handing me my letters, dismissed me with a curt "Good afternoon."

Once out of the apartment I was, I confess, assailed with an awful feeling of apprehension. Here obviously was an intensely irritable, erratic and terrifying personage, who demanded perfection of those who worked for him and *I* was to start my career as his private secretary in a foreign country where all of his settled habits of life would be completely disrupted. To make matters worse I had not taken any dictation for some time and my shorthand was rather rusty. I began to quail at the thought of what Mr. Churchill would have termed "the grievous tribulations" in store for me.

The day that my new employer was due to return from his three-weeks convalescence in Nassau I went to the same Tower apartment and sat down in the crowded little office—which was really a maid's room—to wait for him.

The big living room looked like an overstocked Park Avenue florist's shop. Everyone who was anyone, including the management, had sent enormous bouquets for Mrs. Churchill and Diana, the beautiful red-haired daughter. We had to requisition every available vase in the hotel to hold the sheaves of roses, the exquisite lilies and the masses of sweet-smelling freesia that the maids were lifting out of their tissue-paper wrappings. There was a box of rare orchids for Diana from one of her many admirers and some brilliant flowering plants for Mrs. Churchill. For Mr. Churchill there was a large, suspicious looking wooden case which I surmised—correctly—to be champagne.

A terrific commotion in the hall outside heralded the Churchills' arrival. Their comings and goings are always accompanied by volcanic disturbances. The door of the apartment was ceremoniously opened by the manager and the Churchill family trooped in, Diana chattering shrilly, Mrs. Churchill telling Mr. Churchill he ought to lie down and Mr. Churchill calling loudly for his mail, his secretary and a Scotch and soda. Wherever we went these were his first three requirements.

A procession of porters and bell boys followed in the rear with innumerable well-worn leather suitcases of all shapes and sizes bearing the initials, W.S.C. Mr. Churchill's and Diana's bags were recognizable by their grotesque bulges—the result of poor Sergeant Thompson's frantic last-minute efforts to leave nothing behind. Mrs. Churchill's luggage had a more elegant appearance and was discreetly protected by beige cloth covers.

Diana clung firmly to a tiny case of lavender colored leather which, I supposed at the time, contained her jewelry but later discovered was her make-up kit. I got to know that wretched case very well. Diana had the deepest affection for it; in her mind it assumed an importance equal to that of the blue dispatch box which her father carried so carefully. Her kit was invariably missing when we were stampeding to catch a train. Sergeant Thompson's repeated efforts to find it while calming Mr. Churchill's impatience and endeavoring to avert hysterics in Diana must have cost that sorely-tried detective-valet-nursemaid more gray hairs than all the criminals in England. To make matters worse the case had a faulty clasp and on several occasions—oddly enough always at a railway station—it flew open scattering a fantastic assortment of toilet bottles and face creams over the platform. Before long it had become a stock joke between Diana and myself.

When the Churchills had made their tempestuous entry, I went into the dining-room with my notebook and sat down at the table opposite Mr. Churchill who was already deep in his mail. Without looking up he began to dictate in his deep resonant voice. This was the first time I noticed his curious habit of whispering each phrase to himself before he says it aloud. I also discovered to my horror that he had a very marked lisp which made certain words impossible to understand. When at last he paused for breath I asked very timidly if he would repeat these words for me. All I got was an impatient growl which decided me to ask no more questions. Thereafter I thought it safer to use my imagination.

My first days with Mr. Churchill were a nightmare of continuous dictation, intimate chatty letters to men and women in English political and social life, the Duke of Westminster, Viscount Willingdon, his cousin the Duke of Marlborough; more formal, detailed reports to members of the government in England on the state of his health, the state of America, his plans for the future; letters to statesmen in India, Africa and Australia; letters to his secretary at Westerham Manor, in Kent, with whom he corresponded almost daily; orders for his estate manager, his lawyers, his political secretary in London.

On Mr. Churchill's behalf I maintained a lively correspondence with one of his secretaries in England. She was entrusted with a hundred and one personal commissions—from paying a bill for Diana to taking care of important business with Mr. Churchill's publishers. In return she kept up a voluminous correspondence with us touching on every detail of Mr. Churchill's affairs at home.

His methods of handling his large correspondence are unique and characteristic of the man. Unlike so many of the statesmen with whom I have worked Mr. Churchill, *before* summoning me to take dictation, would go carefully through his mail, size up the contents of each letter and plan the gist of his replies. He dictated slowly and deliberately, whispering phrases to himself and testing several alternatives aloud before making his final choice. His thoughts never wandered from what he was doing. He took incredible pains with his correspondence so that once a letter was finished there was rarely any need for revision or correction. He never fumbled or asked, "What did I say?" and seldom asked to have a letter read back to him when he had finished dictating.

Churchill betrayed only one form of carelessness, an indifference to the subtle technicalities of etiquette in addressing people with titles and honors. Mrs. Churchill would often rush anxiously into my office after reading the carbon of some letter I had just typed to change an "Honorable" to a "Right Honorable" or to make sure that a foreign dignitary had been credited with his full complement of titles.

"Winston is so careless about these things," she would say apologetically when a letter had to be retyped. "But I do think they're important. People's feelings are so easily hurt." Mrs. Churchill incidentally had an encyclopedic knowledge on the subject of addressing the peerage.

After some practice I found it was not difficult to keep pace with Mr. Churchill's dictation. It was when I went off to start typing that the pressure became so frantic. A few minutes after I had got back to the cramped little office, now once again cluttered up with the family trunks and suitcases, and started to pound feverishly at my typewriter Sergeant Thompson would appear to ask me, in an apologetic tone of voice, whether the letters Mr. Churchill had dictated were ready for his signature. To add to my troubles I would be interrupted by an endless succession of telephone calls or requests to look up numbers for Mr. Churchill. He would never approach the receiver unless he was sure the party he was calling was ready to talk to him at the other end. The idea of waiting a few seconds for an answer was unthinkable to him but like so many impatient people he did not in the least mind keeping others waiting.

Sergeant Thompson, who had a little office near mine, seemed to be just as busy as I was. He would dash in and out to look up an address, to dive into a trunk for some piece of clothing that was wanted, to fetch a book or to say would I please hurry with the letter to so-and-so as it simply must catch the next mail. Most of the time it seemed that the fate of nations depended on our catching the next mail!

It didn't take me long to discover that to Winston Churchill a secretary is a completely impersonal adjunct, a machine that must have no personal needs—for food, rest or recreation, somebody who must be on call when he wants them, a being anonymous, perfectly efficient and completely dedicated to the service of Winston Churchill.

Nevertheless, he seems to cast a spell on you that quite reconciles you to his exacting demands on your endurance, his terrifying impatience and unpredictable fits of irritation. I somehow felt that this man had a direct hand in shaping the world's affairs and that, in a very small way, I was being taken behind the scenes and allowed to share in the work. It was exciting and, I must confess, satisfying to the ego. I think that is the reason why very few secretaries—and Mr. Churchill has employed a good number of them in his time

—have left his service except to get married or retire.

I have never worked so hard or so fast in my life. I would fill two shorthand notebooks in the course of a day. I always carried at least half a dozen pencils and an extra notebook with me when I went in to take dictation. Nobody bothered to ask me if I had had lunch and sometimes in the middle of the afternoon a sharp pang of hunger would remind me that I had eaten nothing since early morning. Then I would gulp down a sandwich and coffee, literally without tasting them, while I went on with my endless typing.

I never seemed able to catch up with my work. Even after dinner, which was served at 8 o'clock, Mr. Churchill would think of still another letter that must be written immediately. By this time it required a superhuman effort to keep track of what he was saying. My mind would be in a daze, my arms and shoulders ached with typing. But a letter to Mr. Lloyd George would remind him that he ought to write to Sir Archibald Sinclair and that would lead to another to his friend, Mr. Bernard Baruch so that it was often midnight before I was free to drop, utterly exhausted, into bed.

On one of these nights of toil I inadvertently caused Mr. Churchill much amusement by a mistake in transcribing my shorthand notes. "In my long career of public *exposition*" Winston had dictated, and I typed it out as "In my long career of public *exploitation*."

"Surely, Miss Moir," he said with a chuckle as he read over the manuscript, "you're being a little unjust to me. A long career of public *exploitation*. Really, really! you're doing me an injustice!"

I confess I was far too tired to care which it was.

As Britain's Prime Minister Mr. Churchill now employs six secretaries. I still think it isn't enough. He could find work for a round dozen. And to complicate matters for *me* there was the feminine side of the Churchill menage.

Diana and I very soon became good friends and she would keep dashing in to chatter excitedly about New York and to consult me about clothes, shops, young men and movies—but especially movies. She and Mrs. Churchill had a passion for "the cinema" and always wanted to arrive just when the feature was starting which involved my pouring over movie time tables while great piles of shorthand notes were waiting to be typed.

The trials and tribulations of living and working with genius are proverbial but I think I had more than my fair share during those first hectic days with Winston Churchill.

*Chapter III*

# I MEET HIS FAMILY

❖

THE BOND between the beautiful gentle Mrs. Churchill and her husband is a close and happy one. Theirs is a perfect love match. Born Clementine Hozier, the beautiful daughter of Colonel Sir H. M. Hozier, of the 3rd Dragoon Guards and Lady Blanche Ogilvy, daughter of the seventh Earl of Airlie, Mrs. Churchill and her twin sister were brought up by their grandmother, the Countess of Airlie. The year of her debut she was considered the belle of the London season. Tall, slender, aristocratic, with a lovely English "schoolgirl" complexion, she very soon attracted the attention of dashing young Winston Churchill, already a veteran of three wars, who was then emerging as a figure in English political life.

But theirs was no hasty marriage. Love plays

queer tricks on people and on Churchill the impetuous, so Diana told me, it acted as a steadying influence. He took a long time to make up his mind—far too long, it may have seemed, to pretty Miss Hozier.

But Mr. Churchill did propose and was accepted. In September 1908 they were married at St. Margaret's Church in Westminster, where for several generations fashionable bishops have been marrying fashionable couples with such pomp and ceremony as the current fashion decrees.

Though Mr. Churchill may have been one of the most eligible bachelors in London, Clementine Hozier, generally described as "the loveliest girl in England," was a fitting consort for any man, and her husband still considers he was the lucky one.

"In September 1908 I married and I lived happily ever after," he says in one of his books.

When Winston Churchill courted Clementine Hozier he was running true to form. She was just such a girl as his own father, Lord Randolph Churchill, had courted some forty years before.

Diana loved to talk to me about her beautiful grandmother who had been the toast of London

in her day. All the Churchills have a great venera-
tion for their ancestors and a strong sense of the
continuity of their name. You can't live with
them very long without yourself becoming in-
trigued by the history of this extraordinary
family.

Sergeant Thompson, incidentally, has made
himself quite an authority on this subject. Scraps
of historical anecdote told me by Sergeant Thompson, and Diana and friends of the family prompted
me into doing a little research of my own. And
what immediately fascinated me was the remarkable similarity between the marriages that all the
Churchills have made. A definite pattern seems
to stand out in the romances of three generations
of Churchills. The men have lost their hearts to
charm, beauty and distinction; the women to dash
and good looks. Every Churchill seems to have
regarded his or her parents as the two most remarkable people in the world.

Mr. Churchill's father and mother first met at
a ball on board the cruiser *Ariadne,* lying at
anchor near Cowes, in August 1873. She was
Jennie Jerome, of New York City, and was spending the summer in Europe with her mother, as

was the habit of fashionable Americans in those days. Her father, Leonard Jerome, had for a time been U.S. Consul at Trieste, then a part of Austria, with the result that Jennie had been brought up in the Paris of Napoleon III.

The city of New York was well acquainted with the name of Jerome. The men were dashing and colorful. The first to make a stir was Larry who loved his sport and took delight in racing his horses along the speedways for bets which he usually won. There was William Travers, District Attorney for New York County.

Leonard Jerome, Jennie's father, inherited a passion for racing and founded the first two great race courses established in the United States—Jerome Park and the course belonging to the Coney Island Jockey Club—thus earning the title of "Father of the American Turf."

The Churchills, for all their aristocratic tradition and antecedents, were not much different in temperament from the Jeromes. I was much amused to learn that the first Winston Churchill was known to his contemporaries and biographers as "brilliant but erratic."

The story of Lord Randolph Churchill's whirl-wind courtship has often been told. He made up his mind to marry the lovely American girl after their first dance and proposed a few days later. He and Jennie were married at the British Embassy in Paris.

In the palatial precincts of Blenheim Palace at Woodstock, the ancestral home of the Duke of Marlborough, a son was born to them. They named him Winston Leonard Spencer Churchill.

Mr. Churchill has always experienced a hero worship for his beautiful mother. "In my childhood she shone for me like the Evening Star," he says in one of his books. "My mother always seemed to be a fairy princess; a radiant being possessed of limitless riches and power. I loved her dearly—but at a distance."

There is a strangely close parallel to this in the respect and admiration that Mr. Churchill's children have always felt for their mother, Clementine Hozier. Diana was always a little awed by

Mrs. Churchill's striking beauty and perfect good taste. And no sooner was Randolph interested in a girl than he would tactlessly suggest: "Why don't you do your hair like my mother does?" or "You know, my mother could really show you how to dress."

And indeed she could. Mrs. Churchill's taste is extravagant, but quite exquisite. She has a penchant for trailing black velvet tea-gowns with a touch of color at the wrist and most of her clothes are designed with flowing classical lines. Her hair is gray and softly waved. She visits the hairdresser almost daily. When she walks her clothes seem to become a part of her. She has the litheness, the extraordinary grace of a magnificent thoroughbred.

One might say of her, as of Jennie Jerome, that "her desire to please, her delight in life" have made her the center of a devoted circle. Kind, gay, intelligent, she is the perfect foil for her restless, dynamic husband and has helped to soften and mature his fiery personality.

Mr. Churchill is quite devoted to her and whenever she is not with him he writes her long affectionate letters every day. If there is a decision to be made Mrs. Churchill is invariably consulted. Working with Mr. Churchill I soon grew accustomed to the cry "Clemmie, Clemmie," which seemed to ring through the apartment all day long. I never heard the Churchills argue or quarrel. Only Mrs. Churchill's mild extravagances— she loves expensive clothes—would occasionally provoke a good-humored outburst from her husband who secretly adored to see his wife exquisitely gowned. "Do you realize how many articles that's going to cost me?" he would protest in a scandalized tone of voice, and Mrs. Churchill would dutifully promise to be more careful in the future.

In the thirty years that she has been Mr. Churchill's constant companion, his critic, his nurse and his devoted wife, Mrs. Churchill has never sought the limelight for herself. She has been content to rejoice in her husband's fame. I suspect that Clementine Hozier heartily endorses the old maxim that a woman's place is in the home, even if she happens to be the wife of the Right Honorable Winston Churchill, Prime Minister of Great Britain. Whenever he can, Mr. Churchill spends a few minutes with her at tea-time and discusses with her whatever is in his mind.

Randolph, now the Honorable Randolph Churchill, M.P., had made a lecture tour in America the year before I first went to work for his father and he left behind him a trail of admiring Junior Leaguers the length and breadth of the U.S.A. Wherever we were, beautiful young things would call on Diana at her hotel to press for news of Randolph. Each one seemed to think that she alone had found the key to his heart. Knowing the waywardness of Randolph's affections, Diana would laugh to me about these little romances. She was inordinately proud of her brilliant, extremely handsome brother.

Randolph has more than a touch of his father's genius as a speaker. He is fluent, polished, always witty and sometimes brilliant. He has an ease of manner greater than Mr. Churchill ever had. No sooner did he reach the age of twenty-one than he plunged enthusiastically into politics and very soon gave proof of an astonishing presence of mind on the platform.

On one occasion during his first election campaign, he was addressing a large and rather rowdy audience in the North of England, and had with some difficulty succeeded in capturing its attention when—very late as usual—in walked Mr. Churchill, Sr., with a group of distinguished statesmen all anxious to support Randolph by their presence. Naturally, the crowd promptly forgot about Randolph and rose in a body to give "Winnie" a rousing welcome. The hubbub lasted for several minutes, long enough for Randolph to lose his hold over his audience, a calamity that unnerves the most experienced speaker. But not Randolph. When all was quiet, he resumed his speech with complete composure. Turning slightly toward the distinguished visitors, he began, "As I was saying when I was so rudely interrupted . . ." And elicited a well-deserved volley of applause that rocked the rafters of the hall.

Randolph, too, has followed the family pattern in love. Shortly after the outbreak of war he married Lord Digby's very lovely and dashing daughter Pamela, who is now the mother of Winston Churchill, Jr. The birth of this young gentleman realized one of Churchill's greatest ambitions; it assured him that someone would carry on his name.

Churchill's second daughter, Sarah, embarked upon a stage career. She appeared briefly in one of Charles Cochran's revues and promptly fell in love with Vic Oliver, an American music hall comedian. In spite of stern parental opposition, she followed Oliver to this country and married him. An odd sequel to the romantic story of Lord Randolph Churchill and Jennie Jerome!

The youngest daughter, Mary, who made her debut last winter, is perhaps the most beautiful and by far the gentlest of the Churchill children. She lives with her parents in London and has so far displayed none of the dash or unconventionality of the others.

Diana is the eldest daughter. She has the lovely lines of her mother's face, the prominent eyes of her father and bright red hair.

For a member of one of England's great families, Diana led a rather harum-scarum life. She always overspent her allowance and was chronically hard up, sometimes with amusing results. Invited one summer to a shooting party in Scotland, she could only afford a second-class sleeping coach which, in England, is shared by two people. Diana had been in bed for some time with her inseparable little victrola and a pile of records beside her when a very large, very fat woman appeared to claim her berth. The first thing the woman did was to step on the precious gramaphone and smash the records.

In Diana the Churchill and the Jerome are perfectly balanced. Often she would spend her vacations in the South of France with her fellow students from the Royal Academy of Dramatic Art in London and would live with them in very simple fashion before going on to spend a week-end on the palatial yacht of her father's close friend, the Duke of Westminster.

Diana is a friendly, warm-hearted, impulsive girl. For a time she was in love with the stage and the movies and was frantic with excitement when Warner Brothers, who had seen her in the newsreel pictures, offered to give her a screen test. Her family, especially her father, was dubious but amused and consented to the test. Unfortunately, the result was disappointing.

Like many English girls, Diana bought clothes that caught her fancy at the moment but generally clashed with her unusual type of good looks. When visiting the United States she had come ill-equipped for the rigors of an American winter, and after she had caught a severe cold, Mr. Churchill asked if I could find her a warm but inexpensive coat.

"Not fur, of course. I can't afford it," he said. "But it might have a bit of fur," he added as an afterthought, with a vague gesture which, I suppose, was meant to convey to me where the "bit of fur" might go. Diana, however, refused to let him buy her a coat. What she really needed, she insisted, was a new evening dress. So she and I went on a shopping expedition in search of a suitable evening gown.

Diana was as excited as a schoolgirl. Mr. Churchill had advanced $30 for the purchase but warned me on no account to go above that figure. Diana tried on dozens of dresses. She was irresistibly drawn to trailing lace gowns of which she already had too many. But fortunately the saleswoman and I, by dint of tact and patience and a little judicious flattery, persuaded her to take a beautiful pinkish-beige satin gown that did wonders for her dazzling white skin and brilliant hair.

That evening I witnessed a charming little domestic scene in which Diana, wearing her new gown, appeared for "dear papa's" inspection. As usual papa was in bed, smoking a cigar and reading the evening newspapers. Like a fussy dowager at a fashion show, Mr. Churchill made his daughter parade up and down, scrutinized her from every angle and even took the material of the dress in his fingers to test its quality. When the parade was over we waited in awful suspense for the verdict and were immensely relieved when Churchill said solemnly, "I heartily approve."

A little while later I was again called upon to assist Diana with her shopping. She had caught another bad cold—perhaps the result of not wisely investing papa's $30 in a warm coat—and was feeling tired and out of sorts. Finding the store terribly crowded she had decided to abandon the struggle; and with typical unconventionality she sat down on the stairs to wait for me, a rather forlorn figure. When I returned about twenty minutes later, she was smiling quietly to herself. "Such a funny thing happened while you were gone," she chuckled. "A very kind-faced woman stopped and asked me if I were ill, and if she might be allowed to help me. Wasn't it sweet of her?" I wonder what the kind-faced woman would have said had she known that the "poor waif" who had aroused her pity was the daughter of Winston Churchill.

Diana's first marriage to the handsome eldest son of the South African millionaire Sir Abe Bailey, in the same St. Margaret's Church in Westminster where her father had married her mother, ended in a divorce. Not long after, when campaigning for her brother, Randolph, in one of his several unsuccessful attempts to win a seat in Parliament, Diana met and fell in love with his successful opponent, a very dashing, distinguished young man named Duncan Sandys. This second marriage has been a great success. Diana's home has become the meeting place of the most brilliant younger figures in English political life.

The Churchills, it seemed to me, are a closely knit family. Although Mr. Churchill is a most genial host with a delightful Old World sense of courtesy toward his guests, he is really happiest in the intimacy of his family circle. In the company of his wife and Diana he displays extraordinary streaks of gaiety. I often interrupted Diana putting on a dancing and singing act for Mr.

Churchill, or Mr. Churchill singing songs for Diana. Together they used to have a rollicking good time.

Mr. Churchill, who detests putting himself out for people, would make extraordinary concessions for Diana. One Sunday night when we arrived at a hotel, Diana was seized with an irresistible desire to go dancing. Alas, it was ten o'clock, it was a Sunday night, and we knew no young men in that particular city. Mr. Churchill, sipping a whiskey and soda in his dressing-gown and slippers, was happily contemplating the prospect of a quiet evening's backgammon when his daughter asked timidly if *he* would take her dancing. A famous band was playing at the hotel cafe, and oh! she so much wanted to hear it. Mr. Churchill stared at her over the rim of his spectacles and got to his feet with a look of indulgent resignation. When they reached the cafe there was no one on the floor. But Churchill is not the man to turn back. Very stiffly, and with an awkward sort of dignity, he piloted his daughter through several foxtrots and a waltz. Dancing, I would say, is one thing at which he definitely does not shine.

Churchill's children worship their celebrated

father but in spite of the gay interludes of song and dance they worship him at a distance—as he worshiped his own parents. They consider "dear papa" the most brilliant, the bravest, the greatest of all men, and they stand in secret awe of him.

Mr. Churchill, in turn, is devoted to his children. He is a strong family man and has always taken a keen interest in Sarah's career on the stage, Diana's clothes and Randolph's political ambitions.

It may seem odd that Sergeant Thompson, of Scotland Yard should make his appearance in a chapter devoted to the Churchill family. But whenever I think of the family I seem to see the Sergeant's tall figure hovering somewhere in the background.

For nearly twenty years Thompson has been Mr. Churchill's "shadow" and he is still on the job. He has guarded Churchill against Suffragettes, Sinn Feiners, Communists, Egyptian nationalists, Indian terrorists and the usual percentage of ordinary lunatics, all of whom shared a common desire to put a violent end to Churchill's career.

The relationship between Mr. Churchill and

Thompson was a curious one. Mr. Churchill, it was easy to see, had a genuine affection for Sergeant Thompson. When I first began working for Mr. Churchill I was utterly amazed at the number of times a day the cry "Thompson" would echo through the apartment. But I soon grew accustomed to it. Churchill couldn't possibly get along without his Scotland Yard "shadow."

In addition to guarding his life, Thompson puts out the right clothes for each and every occasion and helps Mr. Churchill into them; he looks up telephone numbers, sees that the book he is reading is always at his side and that he gets to his appointment not more than half an hour late; he finds his spectacles when they are misssing, sharpens his pencils, fills his fountain pen and mixes his highballs. He is literally Mr. Churchill's right hand.

Thompson understood and loved Mr. Churchill. He never flattered him and was not in the least afraid of him. His compelling sense of duty enabled him to get away with what otherwise might have seemed impertinence and he derived an innocent sense of importance from giving Mr. Churchill orders which Mr. Churchill—because he trusted Thompson's wisdom and devotion— generally obeyed without a murmur.

Thompson served Mr. Churchill in the dual capacity of valet and bodyguard during his American visit. He obviously knew nothing about the duties of the first and because of this Mr. Churchill usually presented an oddly crumpled appearance. When traveling, Thompson had a distressing habit of stuffing clothes into a bag and hoping for the best. The art of folding a suit for packing was, not surprisingly, something entirely outside his ken.

Toward the other members of the Churchill family, Thompson's attitude was quaintly fatherly. He was called upon to do all sorts of things for them. If Mrs. Churchill lost her keys, or Diana couldn't close her bulging suitcase, Sergeant Thompson would be summoned to the rescue. His manner was often blunt to the point of rudeness but his devotion to Mr. Churchill excused everything. Should anyone say a word against him, the whole of the Churchill family would fly to his defense, however irritating they might personally have found his behavior.

I found myself doing the same thing. Thompson's unfailing kindness, his sympathy, his unselfish efforts to be helpful in every contingency, have left a very warm spot in my heart for him. Time and again he came to the rescue when I was stumped by a name or a word that Mr. Churchill's haste had left incomprehensible. Thompson was literally our Guardian Angel—cheerful, long-suffering, but amazingly efficient. It makes me happy to think that this man who has for years served Mr. Churchill so faithfully and so well should now in a small way be sharing the limelight with him.

*Chapter IV*

# HOW HE LOOKS AND ACTS

❖

I HAVE ALWAYS FOUND Mr. Churchill in the flesh smaller and rounder than in his pictures. He has the face of a good-humored bull dog. It is a most photogenic face. When dozens of snapshots of him were being examined recently, for a poster, it was discovered that any one of them would be suitable. They were all photographic successes and few of them were posed pictures.

When something amuses Mr. Churchill—and he finds life highly entertaining—the corners of his mouth pucker up roguishly, his rather prominent, blue eyes pop amusingly out of his head and his round, pink face lights up with an impish grin. When he is angry his scowls are prodigious. He reminds one irresistibly of the proverbial bear with the sore head and woe betide anyone who crosses his path on such occasion.

I shall never forget the unfortunate club-woman who buttonholed him in the lobby of a hotel to request his presence at some trifling function. She, poor unsuspecting creature, hit upon him when he was feeling out of sorts. So ferocious was the expression that came over his face when she addressed him that she turned and fled without waiting for an answer. This event immediately put Mr. Churchill in a high good humor.

I remember too the startling case of the intruding reporter. Diana and I were having dinner together in her room when Mr. Churchill burst in on us looking rather dishevelled and extremely annoyed.

"Miss Moir," he said, shaking his finger at me reprovingly, "you should have been with me to protect me. Some rude fellow forced his way into my room." Then, with an unmistakable chuckle, he added, "I'm afraid I had to knock him down. Will you please ask Sergeant Thompson to have him taken away."

Mr. Churchill's appearance is inclined to be sloppy but not for want of valeting. His suits are cleaned and pressed every day and his shoes are carefully shined. It is simply that he has a knack for looking crumpled.

In his salad days, so people say, his taste in clothing leaned toward the eccentric. He would often wear a black waistcoat with a tailcoat and white tie at dinner and when he was made Privy Councillor in 1907 he called on King Edward in a morning coat instead of a frock coat. Today Mr. Churchill's style of dressing is in the main conventional and rather old-fashioned. His lounge suits are dark gray, dark brown and navy blue, usually with a pinstripe. In London he wears a black coat and gray striped trousers and curious buttoned boots with light cloth tops.

Everything in Mr. Churchill's wardrobe is plain but of the very best quality. Even the hideous assortment of gray and black felt hats which, thrust carelessly onto his large head assume an odd chimney-pot appearance, come from the best hatter in London.

Churchill wears fine-spun, cream colored silk pajamas, white silk shirts, silk underwear—here he allows himself a dash of color and favors pink for his shorts—and gray, black, brown or navy blue silk socks, always decorously held up by garters. His handkerchiefs are of silk or very fine linen; his favorite gloves of gray suede. He invariably wears bow ties, usually of a polka-dot pattern that matches the suit he has on.

He is completely devoted to a long, heavily lined, black overcoat with a resplendent astrakhan collar. When I first made its acquaintance it already had a greenish tinge of age. I saw in a picture recently that Mr. Churchill is still wearing it. He was wearing it, and a silk top hat into the bargain, thirty years ago when, as Home Secretary, he led the famous siege on a house in Sidney Street, London, believed to be the headquarters of "forty desperate anarchists." This coat, and the buttoned boots which I always associate with Central European diplomats, form the most incongruous contrast with Mr. Churchill's unique headgear.

His wing collars are almost as famous as his hats. A men's fashion editor wrote of them, "It was a wing collar, but such a wing! Starting to turn back at the front button, these wings kept winging their way back until they finally reached the top of the collar well back of the wearer's ears."

Every night of his life Mr. Churchill dresses for dinner. He dawdles over his dressing and likes to have friends around to talk to or a secretary to dictate to as he ties his tie and puts the finishing touches to his toilet.

Mr. Churchill's gold-rimmed reading spectacles which he wears precariously perched on the end of his short, stubby nose, have been the cause of infinite distress to Sergeant Thompson and to his secretaries who are called upon to find them at a moment's notice when he has absent-mindedly mislaid them—as he is always doing. Unlike so many English gentlemen of the Old School he has never affected a monocle.

Across his waistcoat front there always hangs a massive gold link chain with a very thin gold watch and a tiny gold pocket knife at the end of it. Out of doors he is seldom without a stick. He collects them as a hobby and has assembled an impressive array of them in the umbrella stand at No. 10 Downing Street. Since the outbreak of war one cane has been specially fitted with a flash bulb for blackouts. Mr. Churchill's favorite is the one presented to him by King Edward VII as a wedding gift "to my youngest minister."

When traveling Mr. Churchill carries enough baggage for a regiment. Our every departure caught poor Sergeant Thompson in the throes of a fearful struggle to cram Mr. Churchill's clothing into the already bursting suitcases. A continuous trickle of packages containing socks, shirts and oddments abandoned in the course of his hurried departures generally follow in Mr. Churchill's trail.

To receive the press Mr. Churchill, like an actor dressing for a part, would always don a dark blue, heavily brocaded silk robe and snakeskin slippers. This gave him an amusingly rakish appearance which, when he visited this country, rather bewildered what Thompson referred to as "those American newshawks" who expected Mr. Churchill to be wearing the formal accoutrements of the typical British statesmen.

Incidentally, the "press" dressing-gown nearly caused a minor international incident at the Copley Plaza Hotel in Boston where the reporters turned out in full force for a prearranged interview with Mr. Churchill at twelve o'clock noon. Mr. Churchill, as usual still in bed, called for his blue silk robe. It was nowhere to be found and a frantic search ensued. All this time the crowd of reporters and cameramen in the passage outside was growing restive at the thought of deadlines and irascible city editors. After opening about every trunk and valise Sergeant Thompson at last discovered the robe in a sadly crumpled condition and handed it to Mr. Churchill who took one look at it and snorted, "This will have to be pressed, Thompson. Please send for the valet and tell the gentlemen of the press they will have to wait a few minutes." (They had already been waiting a good twenty minutes.)

Thompson did as he was told and succeeded admirably in further irritating the justly indignant journalists. Only Mr. Churchill's boisterous good humor when the interview finally took place averted another of the fiascoes that have resulted from encounters between visiting British statesmen and the American press. As it was, one enterprising reporter discovered from the hotel valet the cause of the delay and wrote an amusing but highly irreverent feature story about it for his newspaper.

Mr. Churchill never really walks. He always seems to canter. (And I soon found myself doing the same thing.) He is always in a hurry but for some mysterious reason can never get to an appointment on time. I was told that as a very youthful Second Lieutenant he was once honored with an invitation to dine with the Prince of Wales, later Edward VII. Even then Mr. Churchill kept his royal host waiting a full fifty minutes. And he has kept everyone waiting ever since.

I have often heard him say, "Unpunctuality is a vile habit," and I believe he has really tried to break himself of it. But I'm afraid this is one thing in which he has been singularly unsuccessful.

Out of a variety of Churchillian costumes and Churchillian attitudes, two tableaux stand out vividly in my mind: Mr. Churchill sunk in the depths of a huge armchair, a little mound of silver-gray cigar ash piled on his well-rounded midriff; and Churchill, the Man of Destiny, standing like a modern Napoleon, his feet slightly apart, his thumbs under the armpits of his vest, a torrent of words coming from his lips.

A third and somewhat irreverent picture of Mr. Churchill mischievously refuses to be forgotten. It is a still life of a plump, middle-aged gentleman looking at an array of bottles of whiskey, brandy, champagne, and liqueurs. When he was in America he liked to have his little stock of bottles so arranged that he could see it from his bed.

One of Mr. Churchill's best paintings is of two bottles of Scotch and brandy—his favorite drinks—enclosing between them a jug of water and two large cut-glass tumblers.

I believe that Mr. Churchill has an exceptionally keen visual sense. He takes an artist's delight in beauty of line and color. When he sees a beautiful woman, his face lights up with pleasure and admiration.

In his youth, Diana once told me mischievously, her father had "a crush" on Ethel Barrymore who was then the toast of London. "Papa besieged her with flowers and notes," Diana said, "and every night he used to go to Claridges for supper where she always went after her performance. But I'm afraid he never got very far. You see Papa was rather shy in those days and Miss Barrymore always had heaps of admirers around her."

On one occasion when Mr. Churchill was passing through Washington, Miss Barrymore happened to be playing in that city. She must have been touched to receive from Mr. Churchill a box of flowers and a note reminding her of a young admirer who used to sup alone in Claridges in the glittering days of Edward VII's London.

Though Mr. Churchill has always been a connoisseur of feminine beauty and elegance, I gathered that he has a low opinion of feminine intellect and derives little enjoyment from conversation with women. This is not surprising in a man who was the sworn enemy of woman suffrage and has vehemently expressed his firm conviction that a woman's place is in the home. Curiously enough the only human being who ever succeeded in frightening Churchill was a woman—by coincidence one I once worked for, the American Mrs.

O. H. P. Belmont, whose daughter married Churchill's cousin, the Duke of Marlborough.

When the Duke and his wife decided upon a divorce, Mr. Churchill was asked to carry out certain delicate negotiations with his cousin's mother-in-law and soon felt the edge of the good lady's notoriously sharp tongue. This formidable female adversary proved too much for him. Probably for the only time in his life he refused firmly to continue the fight. There was obviously no love lost between these two stormy personalities. Mrs. Belmont was an ardent supporter of the English suffragettes and always referred to Mr. Churchill as "that dreadful man."

The omnipresence of American women secretly distressed Mr. Churchill immensely. He once remarked to me that the American scene was "too cluttered up with women." "They are everywhere. They control eighty per cent of the country's wealth. They wield enormous power—and they bully their husbands! The funny thing is," he added, "that American men seem to like it. They just can't live without women all around them."

It was Churchill, the Conservative, the English

aristocrat speaking. But there is in Mr. Churchill just as much of Jerome, the American, as of the Churchill. Unlike most Englishmen, he is naturally at his ease among Americans, who seem to understand him better than his own countrymen. Americans who have spent a week-end at Churchill's country home at Westerham are always astonished and touched by the warmth of his welcome and by the pains he takes to make their visit a memorable one.

His perpetual haste, his keenness, his unconventionality, his natural aptitude for self-advertisement—someone once said "Churchill attracts the limelight like a lightning conductor attracts lightning"—show how strong is the American strain in his blood. During a short stay at the British Embassy in Washington these American characteristics were particularly noticeable.

The Embassy is a beautiful Queen Anne mansion, designed by Lutyens, standing in its own spacious grounds at the far end of Massachusetts Avenue. From the ceaseless stream of traffic that flows along this busy thoroughfare you step into the stately peace of an English country manor. The beautiful double stairway that leads up from the front door, the line of handsome footmen in their scarlet and gold liveries, the endless vistas of crimson carpeted corridors, the neat, efficient maids who arrive each morning at your bedside with clock-work punctuality bearing your breakfast tray, the old-fashioned wardrobes that threaten to collapse on your head when you fumble for your clothes on the old-fashioned hooks, the omnipresent tea tables, the dainty English cakes and scones, and wafer-thin bread-and-butter, the subdued, respectful voices of the servants, the sense of ordered dignified routine that pervades the whole establishment—these hundred and one tokens of English gentility would tame the most unruly schoolboy and put him on his very best behavior. But not Mr. Churchill!

Into this temple of decorum he plunged with that disturbing exuberance which shatters the most time-honored traditions. His habit of working in bed all morning, the mad rush to dress for lunch with the Ambassador—Mr. Churchill was always at least fifteen minutes late—the stream of visitors, the endless telephone calls to his publishers in New York, Randolph at Chartwell, his Parliamentary secretary in London, the endless telegrams, all the cataclysmic disturbances that are an inevitable part of the Churchill's life, were a shocking strain on the solemn hospitality of His Majesty's Embassy in Washington.

At first the staff was horrified by these goings-on. Then they were merely appalled by the variety and complexity of Mr. Churchill's requirements and finally converted, as if by some invisible force, into willing cooperation with the "New Order." The entire life of the household soon began to revolve around him. (And I have seen this happen wherever he is staying.) A perpetual stream of servants with trays and newspapers, messenger boys with telegrams and secretaries with letters, dashed obediently to and fro at his imperious command. Even the Ambassador, Sir Ronald Lindsay, a towering majestic figure of a man—the tallest diplomat then in the service—would come to call on Mr. Churchill in his bedroom after breakfast to consult about the day's activities.

These two made the oddest contrast, the immensely dignified diplomat standing extremely ill at ease at the foot of the old-fashioned four-poster and the Peter Pan of British politics sitting up in bed, a cigar in his mouth, his tufts of red hair, as yet uncombed, scanning the morning newspapers.

In another room along the corridor Diana would be telephoning friends in her shrill penetrating voice, making excited plans for the day. She, too, did her bit to shock this little corner of England by executing a wild Highland Fling in the hall on the night of her arrival.

The schoolboy in Mr. Churchill enjoyed the situation enormously. One morning he put his head around the door of my sitting room with a mischievous grin on his face. "I've done something really dreadful, Miss Moir," he said with mock concern. "I've just asked the Washington exchange operator for a glass of sherry, thinking that I was speaking on the house telephone. I'm afraid I gave her rather a shock."

I couldn't help feeling when we left that in spite of the very courteous farewells everyone in the Embassy was vastly relieved to see a procession of cars carry the Churchills away.

*Chapter V*

# HE MAKES LIFE EXCITING

❖

WHATEVER MR. CHURCHILL is working at—a letter, a speech or an article—he is always in a desperate hurry. The slightest delay irritates him beyond measure. In front of a woman he would never give vent to any word stronger than an impatient "damn," but I have heard tell he has a soldier's command of profanity. He will, however, when put out, mutter angrily to himself and I have even seen him stamp his feet like a spoiled child. I must confess I was quite terrified the first time I witnessed one of these explosions.

We had just returned from the country and Mr. Churchill immediately put through a business call to his publisher. A question arose that could only be answered by consulting a manuscript buried in one of the suitcases which a porter was at that very moment carrying into the next room. Mr. Churchill called to me to bring him the manuscript and since I was by this time quite used to attempting the impossible I merely motioned to the porter to open the case and dived into it, hurling books and papers in all directions until I came across the missing papers at the very bottom. By this time such frantic shouts were coming from the other room that Sergeant Thompson rushed out of his den with a very startled look, imagining no doubt that someone was after his charge's life. I did not pause to explain the cause of the commotion but dashed down the corridor clutching the precious document. Mr. Churchill was standing by the telephone, his face very red and very angry, stamping his feet and spluttering with rage. He literally tore the paper from my hand and, savagely snatching up the receiver from the table, stammered an incoherent answer into the mouthpiece.

I was frankly unnerved and fully expected him to turn on me wrathfully as soon as he had finished. Instead he looked at me rather sheepishly and in a very penitent tone of voice enquired kindly whether I had enjoyed our stay in the country.

As a matter of fact he was always very penitent after such outbursts. Mr. Churchill is not the sort of man to apologize to anyone but he would go out of his way to say something appreciative and his whole manner made you feel he was ashamed of his bad behavior.

This irritability was compensated by his keen appreciation of good service. He was lavish with his praise and you could be quite sure it was sincere. "You're really splendid" or "That was beautifully done," he would say to me when particularly pleased with something I had done. After trying me out with a few letters to see what I could do he turned over to me his run-of-the-mill correspondence to which he merely signed his name.

Here I found my experience with other British statesmen quite invaluable. I was familiar with diplomatic style and blithely composed messages to the Boy Scouts of America, the British War Veterans and innumerable groups and societies.

To most men their correspondence is an irksome duty. For Mr. Churchill—I refer of course to his personal letters—it was a literary pleasure. Those letters of his were little essays, masterpieces of wit and wisdom, tinged with the ceremonious formality of an 18th century nobleman. Such phrases as "most grieved," "highly diverted," "sorely tried," "depressed in spirit" or "keenly elated" would roll sonorously from his lips.

In these epistolary compositions Mr. Churchill would range brilliantly over the wide field of his interests, from poetry to politics, Gandhi to gastronomy. He would pass from rhapsodic comment on the excellence of a dish of oysters to fierce denunciation of a political policy he opposed. He would sketch, in a few deft phrases, a sharply original profile of a new acquaintance or elaborate in several pages of rolling phrases his estimate of some politician. The style was the man—individual, rounded, colorful, unpredictable.

In my association with other statesmen I generally came to anticipate what they would say. Their letters followed a more or less well defined pattern. But with Mr. Churchill the element of surprise was always present and this, I think, is one of the distinguishing marks of his writing. Mr. Balfour and Lord Cecil wrote purer, more

classical prose. I remember especially an exquisitely perceptive portrait of the French statesman,
Aristide Briand, dictated to me by Lord Cecil. It
was a literary work of art as distinguished as the
best that Churchill has produced. But even in
this, and certainly in Mr. Balfour's style, there was
lacking the intense aliveness, the elemental force
that today enables Mr. Churchill to stir the hearts
of all English-speaking people with his words.

Mr. Churchill, whose mind is at its keenest
when his body is perfectly comfortable and re-
laxed, works best in bed, a fat cigar clamped
between his teeth, surrounded by the latest newspapers, a pile of books, and the famous blue
dispatch box that carried England's budget for
five consecutive years.

This dispatch box was the only thing that Mr.
Churchill almost invariably carried himself. It
was always locked and the key hung on a massive
chain that was mysteriously attached to his person.
I had been with him for some time before he
paid me the compliment of entrusting it to me.
This occurred when we were attending a large
luncheon party and even then he came over to
warn me to take great care of it. I used to wonder

what made it so precious; the only precious things in it, so far as I could see, were the manuscripts of some speeches—and of these we always had duplicates.

One day I learned from Sergeant Thompson the quaint origin of Mr. Churchill's feelings toward the dispatch box. As Mr. Churchill's bodyguard, Thompson had for several years been in the habit of carrying the blue box to the House for him. On the morning when Mr. Churchill was to read his first budget as Chancellor of the Exchequer, Thompson was as usual going to pick up the dispatch box when Mr. Churchill stopped him.

"No, Thompson," he said, "I am the proper person to guard this little box."

From then on he has never let it out of his sight. After having spent almost the whole of his adult life in the counsels of His Majesty's Government, including five years as Chancellor of the Exchequer, it is not perhaps surprising that Mr. Churchill, even out of office, should have endowed his private papers with great importance.

The old blue dispatch box has come into its own again. Its intricate lock now protects the vital wartime secrets of the British Empire. The war has not changed Mr. Churchill's habits of work. He gets to No. 10 Downing Street around 7:30 in the morning. The Cabinet thought it too dangerous for him to sleep there after the night raids on London began. Exactly where he does sleep when in town is a closely guarded Cabinet secret. Upon arriving at No. 10 Churchill goes down to the heavily reinforced cellar in the basement where he immediately undresses and gets back into bed. He eats a hearty breakfast—in England he starts the day with fruit, cereal and lightly-done eggs or game—reads the newspapers carefully, then turns to the old blue dispatch box and dictates until late in the morning. For the sheer enjoyment of it he occasionally rattles off a magazine article. The by-line, "Winston Churchill," is a familiar sight in English papers and periodicals.

As Prime Minister and First War Lord of Britain, Mr. Churchill has to be up and dressed at 11:30 each morning for a meeting of the Cabinet. He shaves himself with a safety razor—quickly but very carefully. At his morning conferences at No. 10 officials gather in the stately book-lined Cabinet Room at the long mahogany table at which the Ministers of the Crown—but no others —are privileged with their own desk equipment. The Prime Minister sits in the center in a chair larger than the rest with its back to the fireplace. On the walls portraits of past Prime Ministers look down solemnly on their dynamic successor who has revolutionized the tempo of life at No.10.

Mr. Churchill dictates again after lunch—unless there is a tour of inspection to be made—but pauses at five to sleep for two hours before dinner. Churchill, like Napoleon, can catnap anywhere at any time of the day or night and awake completely refreshed. After an exhausting journey the first thing he does is to go to bed and sleep for an hour or so. It has the same effect on him as a full night's rest. Without this fortunate ability to replenish at will his store of energy whenever it is running low Mr. Churchill would never have achieved half of the things he has packed into his staggeringly busy life.

After dinner he returns to his desk and works until two or three in the morning. He never sleeps more than seven hours out of the twenty-four. His whole life is given to the task of winning the war.

In peacetime Mr. Churchill used to soften the transition from pajamas to street clothes by dashing around in shorts and undershirt and a bright red cummerbund while I trotted behind him from room to room with a pad and pencil struggling to keep pace with the torrential flow of words.

Even when Mr. Churchill is in the bathtub there is no respite for his secretary. Occasionally he would call loudly for me to take dictation behind the slightly open door through which he would suddenly appear, a towel draped around his midriff, and roll off in that booming voice of his the last paragraphs of a speech he was to deliver somewhere that evening. Incidentally, this Churchillian habit has caused distress in English country houses where nervous housemaids have been scared out of their wits by the spectacle of a rotund, middle-aged gentleman dashing down a corridor draped in a bath towel.

My association with Mr. Churchill convinced me that the quality most responsible for the man's prodigious achievements is his unflagging zest for creative work.

He is generally depicted as an impatient, erratic genius and temperamentally he is. Intellectually he is a genius that is neither impatient nor erratic but only those close to him have seen this side of the man—the conscientious, prodigious and orderly worker. Mr. Balfour, Lord Robert Cecil and Sir Eric Drummond were all men with a reputation for thoroughness and solidity. But in Mr. Churchill's attention to detail, his infallible accuracy, his infinite capacity for taking pains, he is second to none of them. His brilliance has blinded people to these more solid virtues.

Time and again I was given reason to marvel at the tidiness of his mind. The idea of one unanswered letter is a nightmare to him. If he awoke in the small hours of the night and suddenly remembered some task left undone he would summon me and immediately start dictating. And while I was struggling to come to life Mr. Churchill would be wide awake, puffing his inevitable cigar, an expression of ferocious concentration on his face.

One instance of nocturnal dictation I shall

never forget. One evening, feeling the first symptoms of a cold, I resolved to take the unusual liberty of going to bed at 10 o'clock and asked Sergeant Thompson to explain my absence to Mr. Churchill.

I was fast asleep. It must have been nearly midnight when Thompson, looking like a ghost himself, woke me up. He had a small glass of brandy in his hand. He had a guilty look on his face that spelled the ruin of my night's rest.

"Mr. Churchill says he's sorry, Miss, that you're not feeling well," Thompson mumbled apologetically, "but would you come and take just one letter for him. It's important and must get off tonight."

There is no arguing with Mr. Churchill so I dressed and went in with my notebook. As usual he was comfortably ensconced in bed, smoking a cigar and reading a book. He immediately began to dictate a letter to the English cartoonist, David Low, asking him please to differentiate his cartoons of Churchill from those of Lord Hailsham, another well-known figure in English politics.

"You make us look exactly alike," he complained good humoredly. "I should be glad if you would do something about it."

I failed completely to see that there was any great rush about this letter but then every letter he writes is to him a matter of the most desperate urgency. If he wants something, however trivial, there is no peace in the household until he gets it.

I remember once on a long train journey Mr. Churchill, after retiring for the night, asked Sergeant Thompson for a certain book he wanted to read. Thompson, almost asleep on his feet at the end of an exhausting day, explained that the volume in question was packed in a trunk that had been checked in the baggage car at the far end of the train. Mr. Churchill asked him to fetch it. Comfortably ensconced in my berth half way down the pullman, I peeped out through the green curtains and watched Thompson stagger off sleepily, thanking my lucky stars that I had escaped this unpleasant little task. After some fifteen minutes he came back to report that the baggage master had refused to let him get at the trunk which was wedged in an inaccessible corner of the tightly packed car. Mr. Churchill, in a loud voice that provoked a chorus of indignant protests from sleepy passengers in the car, instructed Thompson to bring the baggage master to him.

Poor Thompson again set out wearily on his long trek up the train and reappeared with the indignant baggage master. The irate official's protests were abruptly silenced when he saw the look on Mr. Churchill's face. There followed a hushed conversation that I could not catch and the two men disappeared. This time—after a much longer interval in which the baggage car was no doubt taken to pieces—Thompson returned triumphantly with the book.

This little incident is characteristic. When Mr. Churchill has an idea he must take immediate steps to carry it out. Thought and action are with him almost simultaneous—and there are no impossibilities.

Today it is as well for England that this should be so.

Mr. Churchill's power of concentration was another source of continual wonderment to me. He has the ability to throw himself completely into whatever he is doing—the preparation of a speech or a friendly game of backgammon—and to achieve a state of childlike absorption. The world around him utterly ceases to exist. He can work as intensely on a rocking transcontinental express as in the quiet of his study at Chartwell and is quite oblivious to the noisy comings and goings of his family.

The day that Prague was seized by the Nazis he was hurrying to complete a 300,000 word history of the English people. After dinner he said to Randolph, "It's hard to take one's attention off the events of today and concentrate on the reign of James II—but I'm going to do it." And he marched to his study on the first floor and began to dictate. Unlike most British statesmen I have known Mr. Churchill genuinely enjoyed working under pressure and I never saw him show any signs of nervous strain.

Many of his problems he solves by arguing the pros and cons aloud to himself. At first I found this curious habit extremely disconcerting. On one occasion, during my first week with him, I heard what seemed to be a heated discussion from the living room where only a moment before I had left Mr. Churchill alone, seated in an arm-chair by the fireplace. Thompson was out to lunch and remembering his warning about unannounced visitors I dashed into the living room. I found him quite alone, pacing up and down the room with his head sunk between his shoulders, talking loudly to himself. He didn't even notice my wild intrusion and I was able to escape an embarrassing explanation. I wonder if, as Britain's Prime Minister, he has taught himself to heed his own wartime slogan: "Beware! Even walls have ears."

His memory is encyclopedic and manifests itself in the oddest ways. I was amused to discover that he knows by heart the words of almost every English musical comedy song-hit of the past twenty years. (He loved to sing them in his booming baritone accompanied by Diana's shrill falsetto.) I reminded him once that on a certain night during the General Strike I had sat directly behind him and Mrs. Churchill in the stalls of a London theatre. Immediately his eyes brightened, his whole face lit up: "I remember," he said excitedly, "I remember perfectly. It was the American play 'Lady Be Good,' with the Astaires. An excellent show." And he gaily broke into one of its hit songs and followed it up with others.

When we visited the battlefields of the Civil and Revolutionary wars Mr. Churchill astonished us all with his knowledge of these campaigns. From his reading he was familiar with every foot of the terrain. At Gettysburg he startled the guide by correcting him as to the disposition of troops and guns. When a checkup was made later Mr. Churchill was proved to have been completely right. He no doubt inherits his amazing memory from his father. Lord Randolph, for a bet, would read through any page of Gibbon's *Decline and Fall of the Roman Empire* and then recite it aloud, word for word, without error.

The keenness of what Stanley Baldwin described as "Winston's hundred horsepower mind" is perhaps in part due to the fact that he never wastes his attention on things that to him are irrelevant. He would testily dismiss as "foolish triviality" gossip, small talk, scandal mongering and the sort of questions that some reporters in search of "human interest" copy were apt to ask visiting celebrities. When interviewed by the press, Churchill was always willing to air his views on world affairs, frankly and at considerable length. But when asked his opinion of "The modern girl" or "career woman" he would explode wrathfully, "Why should I comment on such tommy rot!" And unless someone tactfully returned to the "condition of Europe" the interview would be at an end.

Mr. Churchill's dislike of triviality should not be mistaken for pomposity or solemnity, two failings from which he has never suffered. When in America he was constantly carried away by schoolboy enthusiasms for all the modern American improvements that contributed to comfortable living. Upon arriving at the hotel on a visit to Cincinnati, the Churchills were assigned to the Presidential suite which the management had thoughtfully filled with huge baskets of flowers.

Mr. Churchill was quite enchanted. "It's gorgeous. It's magnificent. It's s-s-simply s-s-splendid," he stuttered—as he always did when excited. The manager, beaming with pride, proceeded to lead the way from room to room explaining all the modern innovations. Mr. Churchill, as happy as a small child in a toy shop, cantered behind commenting enthusiastically on the arrangement of the rooms, the furnishings and the lighting fixtures. When we reached the master bathroom Mr. Churchill, quite carried away by the effect of the colored fixtures, darted to the nearest telephone and to everyone's amazement asked to be put through to London.

"I'm calling the designer who's remodeling my country house at Chartwell," he explained. "I want him to suspend operations on the bathrooms until I reach home. I'd like to have this copied."

"Operator, operator," he growled impatiently, looking anxiously at his watch. "Hurry that London call through, please. It's terribly urgent." It was twelve noon in Cincinnati, 5 P.M. London time.

"I do hope he hasn't left the office yet." Then, with an exclamation of delight: "Hello. This is Mr. Churchill speaking . . . I'm quite well, thank you. Listen carefully, please. I want you to suspend operations on the bathrooms until I get back. I've seen something here that is most unusual in bathroom decoration, and I want to work out some ideas it has given me for our new bath.

I can't tell you or write you, so please do nothing until my return. That's it. Nothing until my return."

The conversation finished, Winston heaved a great sigh of relief. He put down the receiver as delighted as if he had averted a major world crisis.

*Chapter VI*

# HE ENJOYS MANY HOBBIES

❖

MR. CHURCHILL'S IDEA of relaxing from politics and speech-making is merely to indulge in different forms of activity which is something that even people who know him well can never understand. I shall always remember one particular week-end as especially characteristic of Mr. Churchill's behavior when he is on holiday.

When Mr. Churchill was last in America, Mr. Bernard Baruch, his best friend in this country, asked him to spend Washington's Birthday and the following week-end at his plantation in South Carolina.

For four days there ensued an intermittent telephonic conversation between Mr. Churchill and Mr. Baruch as to whether I should accompany Mr. Churchill to the plantation. Mr. Baruch was careful to explain that I personally would be very welcome but that he felt my presence would give Mr. Churchill a plausible excuse to work. Mr. Churchill insisted that he wouldn't know what to do without a secretary. He had taken one to Scotland in the shooting season, to the Riviera in the gambling season and to Morocco in the yachting season. A secretary was as necessary to him as a fountain pen. (As a matter of fact, a secretary is the same thing to him as a fountain pen!)

"Besides, my dear fellow," Mr. Churchill argued, "that kind of work—(he had agreed to write a series of articles for *Collier's*) is a relaxation. I enjoy it."

As usual he won hands down. I went.

On the long drive to Georgetown we passed the house of Robert Goelet. He and his wife happened to be standing on the lawn as we went by and Mr. Baruch stopped the car and called to them. They came over and Mr. Churchill was introduced. In the middle of the conversation that ensued he suddenly exclaimed, "Why we must be related. Your sister married a cousin of mine, the Duke of Roxburgh." It turned out that they were.

I mention this little incident because the same thing happened wherever we went in America. Churchill is related to three-quarters of the English peerage and through them and his American mother he has a host of connections in the United States.

Mr. Baruch's vast plantation was situated on an island some miles up the James River from Georgetown. There were no telephones and no means of communication with the mainland except by motor boat. A spacious, rambling colonial house overlooking the river invited the visitor to forget the outside world. The soft southern air had an immediately relaxing effect. The gentle lapping of the water under the windows and the dry rustle of the palmetto trees were the only sounds that broke the silence. It was a haven of peace—the sort of place where work of any kind seemed a sacrilege. But we had no sooner arrived when Mr. Churchill called for me to take a letter. He was already bursting to tell his wife who was in New York his first impressions of the plantation.

I was pleasantly surprised to learn the next day that a riding party had been arranged for Diana and myself by Mr. Baruch's handsome daughter Belle, a famous horsewoman who had won prizes for riding at all the principal horseshows in Europe. To avoid the intense heat of the early afternoon we decided to set out at four.

As we were marshalled in front of the porch before starting Mr. Churchill came out to review us. I have done a fair amount of hunting at various times in my life and naturally have a pretty good seat on a horse. When Mr. Churchill noticed this a look of amazement came over his face. I had no time to think about it because just then we moved off toward the swampy wooded land of the island. The soft sandy paths that ran through long avenues of trees festooned with streamers of pale green moss were perfect for a smooth, gentle canter and I couldn't help noticing that Diana had a very poor seat. She must have been aware of this because she apologetically confessed she'd never been able to afford a thorough course of lessons. The ride was so delightful that we lost all sense of time, and long shadows were falling as we got back to the house.

I hurriedly changed and flew to Mr. Churchill's living room with a notebook, fully expecting to find him fuming about my absence. Instead I noticed a change in his manner toward me. Hitherto he had treated me with complete impersonality as though I were a machine that took down symbols in shorthand and transcribed them with a typewriter into words and letters. But now, glancing up at me approvingly, he said, "You really have a splendid seat on a horse, Miss Moir. I must congratulate you." I think he had suddenly realized I was a human being.

On that week-end at the Baruch's Mr. Churchill did, as a matter of fact, manage to modify somewhat his normal busy routine. He went crabbing with his host, spent part of the mornings discussing world affairs on the sunny terrace, painted several landscapes and played more backgammon than usual. But in the three days we were there he drafted his series of articles for *Collier's,* dashed off another article for a British newspaper and dictated a score of letters. That is Mr. Churchill's idea of a "holiday."

Painting seemed to me to be Winston Churchill's favorite form of relaxation. Wherever he goes he carries a portable painting easel with him as other men carry a set of golf clubs. I once asked Sergeant Thompson how it was that Mr. Churchill had taken up this hobby.

"Well, Miss," he said, "it was after that shocking business at Gallipoli. Mr. Churchill was very hard hit. The papers, you know, were pretty nasty about it. Any other man would have gone off the deep end. But not Mr. Churchill, Miss. He's one not to cry over spilt milk. You simply can't down him. He just looks around for something new to turn his hand to. So one fine day he started painting."

From several conversations with Sergeant Thompson and Diana I learned the rest of the story. Shortly after the Gallipoli fiasco Mr. Churchill bought a complete painting outfit, donned a smock—for he has to dress up for a new role—and sat down in front of an easel in the country. But Mr. Churchill never does anything by halves. If he was to be an amateur in painting he must at least be a distinguished amateur. Besides, as I often heard him say, to get the greatest enjoyment out of anything you have to do it well. So he turned to his friend, the famous British artist, Sir John Lavery, for lessons. Under Lavery's guidance Mr. Churchill's artistic talent unfolded rapidly. His pictures, signed "Charles Marin," were singled out for praise at a Paris Exhibition where they sold for $150 apiece. On one occasion he and his teacher painted the same landscape and anonymously submitted their work to a group of critics. Churchill's was acclaimed the better!

In painting Mr. Churchill found the perfect outlet for his creative energy. "It is a delightful amusement," he says. "It would be a pity to shuffle through one's playtime with golf and bridge when there is close at hand a wonderful new world of art and craft."

The habit, once formed, remained with him for life. He has painted landscapes in the South of France; he has painted the canal land of Holland, the Fjords of Norway, the monuments of Ancient Greece, the Rocky Mountains and the plantations of South Carolina. When he toured Egypt as Home Secretary he took time off to paint the Pyramids.

This latter picture has an amusing story attached to it, related to me by Sergeant Thompson.

Mr. Churchill made his first attempt perched on a camel—but promptly fell off. The second time he adopted a more orthodox position but soon attracted the attention of a group of English soldiers who gathered curiously around him. Disturbed by Mr. Churchill's impetuous technique, one of them expostulated: "Blimey, Sir, you don't arf put the paint on. Now, if you was an 'ouse painter with me old foreman, you wouldn't 'arf cop it."

Mr. Churchill turned round and eyed the speaker with a broad grin. "Gawd," the critic exclaimed in horror. "It's Winston." But Mr. Churchill soon dispelled his anxiety and then turned to finish the picture.

As a matter of fact the Tommy's comment was fully justified. Someone has aptly remarked that Mr. Churchill's strong sense of color leads him to assault a canvas with more exuberance than discretion. Again the style is the man—brilliant, erratic, rather overwhelming. To hang his paintings Mr. Churchill has built, with his own hands, a miniature gallery on the grounds of his Manor House at Chartwell. There his brilliantly colored canvases were hung on the walls, a permanent one-man show to which all of his guests are taken on their conducted tours of the estate.

Mr. Churchill took up bricklaying, his other favorite hobby, after another political crisis which excluded him from the government. He had recently purchased Chartwell Manor in Kent on the proceeds of his book *The World Crisis*. Black swans for the lake were imported from Australia, a heated swimming pool was installed for the guests and a warm water pond for the goldfish.

The other embellishments Mr. Churchill set about building with his own hands. He built artificial dams, rock gardens and miniature waterfalls. He built the cottages and the garden walls. He even forced his week-end guests to don overalls and assist him. For the good of their souls, he said. When the bricklayers' union protested against his non-union labor he solemnly filled out a union card and applied for membership. He was accepted and duly paid his subscription of five shillings by check.

I wonder whether he is still a member of that union.

Bricklaying, I feel, has filled what might have been the only gap in Churchill's life, his need for some form of manual labor. As a boy, he says, he would have preferred to work in the fields or learn some craft rather than go through the normal education of an English gentleman. Like most men of genius he likes to work with his hands.

Mr. Churchill has a number of other hobbies. When he was younger—and much lighter—he rode, swam, played a first-class game of tennis, hunted big game, rode to hounds and played polo. In all of these sports he has distinguished himself. At Harrow he won the Public Schools fencing championship. He flew a plane in the days when every flight was a highly risky adventure and has crashed often. He played polo, with an injured right arm strapped to his side, in the 4th Hussars team that won the coveted Championship of the Indian Army. But riding has always been his favorite sport.

"Don't give your son money," he counsels parents. "Give him horses. No one came to grief, except honorable grief, through riding. No hour of life is lost that is spent in the saddle. Young men have often been ruined through owning horses or through backing them; but never through riding them; unless, of course, they break their necks which, taken at a gallop, is a very good death to die."

In his maturity Mr. Churchill has taken up less strenuous diversions. He is—I have been told by people who played with him—a good backgammon player and takes huge delight in outwitting his opponent. In peacetime he used to enjoy a flutter at the tables at Le Touquet. He is a keen tennis fan and has regularly attended the championship matches at Wimbledon. Mrs. Churchill plays an excellent game and her husband loves to watch her.

Mr. Churchill prides himself on his cooking. As a soldier of the Empire he frequently had to prepare a rough and ready meal over a camp fire. Nowadays he is content to do a cutlet or a sausage to a nice turn over the electric grill at Chartwell. But as a mark of esteem for specially privileged guests he will map out with them and cook with his own hands a whole dinner.

The theatre is Mr. Churchill's oldest love. He has always been an assiduous theatregoer. His taste is, as in all things, catholic, but here he leans slightly toward the frivolous. He goes to the theatre to be entertained and loves gay, sparkling revues and musical comedies. He has not missed a musical hit in years.

Conversation, I have always felt, is to Mr. Churchill something akin to a hobby, one which he enjoys keenly. To hear him talk, and he talks a great deal, reminded me of the vanished age when conversation was considered the highest of all arts. Mr. Chenery, editor of *Collier's Magazine,* said to me quite recently: "I have never in my life heard anyone talk as well as Churchill. Only Elihu Root and Newton D. Baker could approach him for amplitude of mind, eloquence and smoothness of finish, and they lacked his fire. His control over thought and feeling and the precision of his language are amazing."

Mr. Chenery recalled one conversation with Churchill which, he said, had held him spellbound. "Churchill began discussing the American standard of living," Mr. Chenery told me. "He declared that if we hadn't made one or two serious economic blunders we could have created a civilization far beyond anything the world had dreamt of. He went on talking in that vein for at least an hour, and I just listened to him fascinated. I had the feeling I was seeing a truly great mind operating under full power, and yet smoothly and beautifully."

The speech of the average Anglo-Saxon, English or American, is halting, confused, incomplete. A sentence is begun and never finished. Ideas are jumbled together without logic or sequence. Not so with Mr. Churchill. His everyday speech is on the same literary and intellectual level as his writing and is richly studded with quotation from his wide reading.

Mr. Churchill is no conservative in the use of language. He is constantly in search of the vigorous, the trenchant, the colorful term and is always willing to blaze new trails. For this reason he heartily approved of many American idioms.

"It's so expressive, Miss Moir," I remember him saying once, when he felt, perhaps, that he ought to justify to an Englishwoman a piece of American slang he had deliberately used in a letter to a British statesman.

The most overworked word in Mr. Churchill's vocabulary is—significantly I think—the word "prod." He was always talking about being "prodded" by doctors, "prodding" Cabinet Ministers, "prodding" his lawyers, publishers and political rivals. Undoubtedly he has prodded the British Empire as it has not been prodded for generations.

Mr. Churchill never talks for the sake of talking. If the conversation sinks to trivialities he relapses into bored silence. But he is always ready to hold forth endlessly on his favorite topics of politics, literature, journalism and Winston Churchill.

He loves especially to reminisce about his boyhood and his army days, how he was a dunce at Harrow, how he escaped from an enemy prison camp during the Boer War and how he was carried into Parliament on the crest of a journalistic scoop. I have even heard him try out on some visitor whose judgment he respected a speech or a lecture he had to deliver.

When Mr. Churchill is annoyed his wit can be sharp and merciless. At a dinner party in England he once got into a heated argument with his cousin, Lord Londonderry.

"Have you read my latest book?" Londonderry asked, hoping to drive home his point.

"No," said Churchill bitingly, "I only read for pleasure or profit." A witness of this verbal encounter laughed heartily as he told me the incident.

This gift for phrase-making on the platform is matched in his private conversation by a terrifying genius for epigram. Of Ramsay MacDonald he once said, "He has more than any other man the gift of compressing the largest amount of words into the smallest amount of thought." And referring to Stanley Baldwin in the House of Commons Mr. Churchill remarked, "He used to be wiser. He used to take my advice." No wonder Baldwin dispensed with his services in the Cabinet. "I make up my mind," he complained to a colleague, explaining Churchill's exclusion from the Government, "then along comes Winston with his hundred-horse-power brain, and makes me change it."

It is not merely Mr. Churchill's hundred-horse-power brain that has enabled him to win people over to his viewpoint. A subtle strategist in all things, he also knows when and how to soften the impact of his personality and turn on his natural charm to make a new friend or appease a rival or an enemy.

Of the many forms that conversation can take I am sure that Mr. Churchill enjoys most a serious heart-to-heart discussion with men of his own intellectual calibre. He has very few such intimates. His busy life and strong family sense have left him little time, and I think little wish, to cultivate deep friendships. Few people can measure up to his requirements. To get along with Mr. Churchill you have to make him respect you. To become his friend you also have to make him admire you, for your character and your intellectual achievements. Mr. Churchill's closest friends —General Sir Ian Hamilton, Lord Birkenhead, Leopold Amery, Mr. Bernard Baruch and "Lawrence of Arabia"—have all had these two things in common.

Mr. Baruch and Mr. Churchill first became acquainted when Mr. Churchill was Minister of Munitions and Mr. Baruch was on the U. S. War Industries Board. Mr. Baruch is one of Mr. Churchill's few intellectual equals. Mr. Churchill had implicit faith in his judgment and in "Bernie's" company he would freely hazard his opinions about the United States, something he was reluctant to do elsewhere. He was intensely interested in America's affairs and his strong tradition of "Tory Democracy" made him feel it was dangerous to provide so little social security for the workers.

The American economic system, I once heard him say to Mr. Baruch, was like an express elevator without brakes. When something went wrong there was nothing to check the rapidity of the descent and sooner or later America would have to expand social security to the same scale as in England.

The friendship between Mr. Churchill and Lord Birkenhead (formerly plain F. E. Smith) was one of the most peculiar phenomena of British political life. Some thirty-five years ago the intellectual brilliance of Mr. F. E. Smith, then the stormy petrel of the Conservative Party, involved him in many sharp clashes with Winston Churchill who was in those days a Liberal with radical leanings. In private life the two soon became boon companions; but they continued for years to oppose each other bitterly in public.

He has never been so closely attached to any other man.

Differences of age have been no barrier to Mr. Churchill's friendships and only death has ended them. Ian Hamilton was twenty years his senior. When the two first met Hamilton was a colonel in the British Army in India, Mr. Churchill only a subaltern.

T. E. Lawrence, "Lawrence of Arabia," was thirteen years Mr. Churchill's junior. They were introduced at the Peace Conference in Paris when Lawrence was slightly out of favor for his championship of the Arab cause and for what officials at the British Embassy considered his "theatrical behavior." He insisted on walking about the streets of Paris in an Arab burnous with a vicious-looking dagger hanging from his crimson belt.

Mr. Churchill, himself a man with an inveterate penchant toward the dramatic, tolerantly overlooked Lawrence's comic opera facade, sensing behind it a brilliant intelligence and statesmanlike grasp of the situation in the Middle East. Two years later, when Mr. Churchill was Colonial Secretary, he remembered the young man he had met in Paris, and summoned him to join the Middle Eastern Department of his Ministry. From then on until Lawrence's tragic death, the two were firm friends and collaborated closely in working out a solution to the tangled problem of a settlement with the Arab leaders.

Mr. Churchill's friendship with Leopold Amery, now Secretary of State for India, had a curious origin. It dates back to his first days at Harrow. Young Winston, taking a small, naked figure standing on the edge of the swimming pool to be that of another schoolmate, could not resist the temptation to push him into the water. The small figure turned out to be that of Leopold Amery, a sixth-former, head of his house, and editor of the school paper. Confronted with this august personage, Winston did not entirely lose his presence of mind.

"My father," he explained apologetically, "who was a very great man, was *also small.*"

*Chapter VII*

## HE IS AN EPICURE

❖

I<small>F</small> M<small>R</small>. C<small>HURCHILL</small> had never been a great statesman and a great journalist he would have found
a little niche in history as an epicure.

When making preparations to receive Mr.
Churchill in America Mr. Alber, his lecture manager, once consulted an official at the British Embassy in Washington about his client's tastes in
food and drink.

"Mr. Churchill's tastes are very simple," the
official replied. "He is easily pleased with the best
of everything."

Mr. Churchill, though never a heavy eater, is
a connoisseur of good food and good wines. But
one cannot exactly call him a gourmet because
he has not the gourmet's love of complicated and
exotic dishes. The first time he stayed at the

Waldorf-Astoria Mr. René Black, an internationally famous maitre d'hotel, presented himself to inquire into the preferences of his distinguished guest.

"Whatever the Good Earth offers, I am willing to take. I am a very simple person," said Mr. Churchill.

But the simplicity he appreciates is the simplicity of perfection, in cooking and in service. To the latter he attaches great importance. "One slice of ham well presented is better than a steak that weighs three pounds," I have often heard him say. He hates the fussy, officious kind of service that is accompanied by a great display of bowing and scraping. "Over-service," in his opinion, "shows a deplorable lack of good taste."

Mr. Churchill eats quickly but savors each mouthful, and dislikes too many courses. "I hate wading through a long dinner," he says. "Give me a few well cooked dishes that I can really enjoy."

He enjoys a perfectly done lamb chop and considers soups "a good culinary institution." He is fond of sea food, especially clams and American oysters which are larger than those in Europe.

When in this country he would often build a whole meal around fish. He insists upon having his meat roasted, because in roasting none of the juices and none of the flavor is lost. I once heard him heartily endorse Savarin's dictum that "Roast cooks are born; sauce cooks are made." But being a philosopher in food as in all things he remembers to eat what is healthy, merely seeing to it that his palate is not offended. He is a firm believer in the sovereign virtues of salads and prepares the dressing with his own hands.

This operation becomes quite a solemn ritual when performed by Mr. Churchill. He gets up from the table and marches ceremoniously to the sideboard. First, he pours the right amount of oil into a small bowl, then sniffs the vinegar judicially and, if it passes the test, he adds the right measure to the oil with pepper and salt to taste. The whole is mixed vigorously and now, according to Mr. Churchill, comes the most important part. He sprinkles the dressing over the salad which he insists on having served in a very large wooden bowl and, with his usual intense concentration, he mixes the whole very thoroughly but very lightly so as not to spoil the freshness of the leaves. He never rubs the bowl with garlic as many epicures like to do. Mr. Churchill continues methodically until satisfied that the dressing has permeated to every leaf. Then, with great pride, he carries the salad bowl back to the table and serves the helpings himself with a large wooden fork and spoon.

He has a special weakness for all kinds of cheese which he likes to eat with his salad. The combination seems to give an added enjoyment to the strong cigars he puffs between mouthfuls. In this too he is a nonconformist. A conventional gourmet would be horrified at the idea of smoking with his food. He always keeps a bowl of fruit in his rooms and will bite into a peach or an apple at odd times of the day or night.

In René Black Mr. Churchill found a culinary artist with whom he could enjoy long conversations on what to him is one of the most fascinating of all subjects. He prefaced their first talk with the remark, "Gentlemen don't have to be ashamed of liking good food," and then plunged into an enthusiastic discourse on gastronomy. He entered into the history of certain dishes and the origins of recipes. He held forth about the great Savarin, the most celebrated of French culinary geniuses. He plied Mr. Black with searching questions about food values and vitamins. Why are green peas always served with lamb and spinach with veal? How do you make Sole Marguery? "Just tell me simply how you do it." But nevertheless he wanted every detail of the recipe, and in layman's language.

"He reminded me of my professor of mathematics at school," Mr. Black told me. "In the history and literature class I could get away with generalizations and small inaccuracies. But when it came to mathematics I was up against it. I had to know my facts and figures. That was what Mr. Churchill was always after. He checked me on everything. He wanted to know sources, history and background. His curiosity simply amazed me."

Like all wise travelers who have cultivated the art of good living Mr. Churchill makes a point of sampling the national dishes of whatever country he is in—frogs' legs in Paris, in Marseilles a Bouillabaisse, strongly flavored curries in India, and in America seafood, especially clam chowder made of Cotuit clams from Boston. At home he eats a hearty English breakfast, in France café-au-lait and a croissant and in the United States orange juice, scrambled eggs and coffee. Very occasionally he takes tea, sometimes in the morning as a change from coffee, sometimes in the afternoon with a petit beurre.

In Paris, Mr. Churchill was a habitué of the Café des Anglais, first made famous by King Edward VII, and of the famous Café Riche on the Boulevard des Italiens. In London, when not dining at home, he is often seen in the best clubs. He belongs to The Turf, the home of the huntin', shootin' and fishin' aristocracy, and to The Atheneum, the mecca of English intellectualism.

The plain but perfectly done chops and steaks in which English clubs excel are much to his liking. Mr. Churchill is one of the world's few gourmets to see virtues in English cooking. "At its best it's about as good as anything you can get," he says patriotically.

Mr. Churchill, always awake early, breakfasts at seven, lunches at one, and dines at eight. Ordering dinner is a solemn ritual from which he derives as much enjoyment as in eating it. His face lights up, his whole personality expands and he concentrates on the menu as though planning an important military campaign. He seems to savor the dishes as he names them and explains very painstakingly how he wants everything done.

Mr. Churchill has a special fondness for picnics, not the rough and ready paper bag affairs, but elaborately prepared little feasts of caviar, cold game, hothouse fruits, and of course, champagne. This once gave rise to an amusing little incident which I witnessed. On one occasion at lunch in a hotel, Mr. Churchill had as usual summoned the head waiter to plan the menu for a picnic that was to take place the next day. After selecting the main items Mr. Churchill, a precise man in all things, set about explaining how the roast beef sandwiches were to be made.

"I want some solid, substantial sandwiches," he announced to the astonished head waiter, as solemnly as though he were making a statement to the House. "Get hold of a large loaf, and don't cut the slices too thin—or too thick, either. Trim the crust off the edges, and put plenty of butter on the bread. Please see to it there's enough beef for us to know it's a beef sandwich. And make certain that the beef comes clear to the edge of the bread. I don't like to bite twice into a sandwich before I can tell what's inside of it."

All this was rattled off with a very pronounced lisp, which left the unfortunate waiter completely bewildered. "Never mind," said Mr. Churchill impatiently, when he realized the man had not taken in a word. "Bring me some paper and a pencil." And then and there he proceeded to illustrate the exact size and thickness of the sandwiches with a series of quick sketches, little blueprints of gastronomical architecture.

Mr. Churchill enjoys a drink. I have noticed that it seems to renew his strength and energy; it brings a sparkle to his eye and added fire to his manner. "You can't make a good speech on iced water," I have often heard him say.

At home or on travel, at work or on holiday, Churchill drinks a glass of dry sherry at mid-morning and a small bottle of claret or Burgundy at lunch. To Mr. Churchill a meal without wine is not a meal at all. When he is in England he sometimes takes port after lunch, and always after dinner. It is at this time that his conversation is most brilliant. In the late afternoon he calls for his first whiskey and soda of the day. Unlike most Englishmen he drinks it with ice. He likes a bottle of champagne at dinner. After the ritual of port he sips the very finest Napoleon brandy. He may have a highball in the course of the evening.

When I was with Mr. Churchill he always traveled with several boxes of long, very strong-smelling and very expensive Havana cigars. He smoked about fifteen of them a day but seldom smoked one to the end. He threw them away after he had got the best out of them. I very rarely saw him without one. Hostesses invariably complained that wherever he went he left behind him a trail of cigar ash on their valuable carpets. I have never seen him smoke a pipe or a cigarette. I can't imagine him doing it.

Mr. Churchill's cigar has taken the place of Chamberlain's umbrella as Britain's national emblem. The pottery works of Stoke-on-Trent are turning out for the American market Toby jugs fashioned into the likeness of the Prime Minister, a cigar clenched between his teeth in such a way as to give him a particularly pugnacious expression. When King George and Queen Elizabeth visited the pottery works the King examined the Toby jugs with critical interest. "I do not think he smokes his cigars at such a low angle," the King remarked earnestly, thereby sending the pottery firm's executives into a hurried conference on the slant of Winston Churchill's cigars.

Mr. Churchill's love of good living seems to have had absolutely no effect on his health other than to add inches to his waistline and his collarband. He has never suffered a pang of indigestion in his life. He is blessed with a positively Herculean constitution. In spite of the terrific pace at which he has lived he can proudly state that now in his sixties he is in excellent physical condition. His blood pressure is practically normal. For some strange reason he rather enjoys having it taken. This is one of his few little foibles.

I found his attitude toward his health extremely sane and quite characteristic of the man. He regards the body as a machine which must at all costs be kept running smoothly. His particular machine will stand a great deal of wear and tear. But if anything does go wrong he promptly consults his doctor and explains his symptoms minutely, with a quite impersonal detachment.

In an old notebook of mine I found the following extract from a letter dictated by Mr. Churchill to one of his physicians when he was convalescing after a serious accident. "I have regained my full mental and physical vigor but I tire more easily. Especially I feel the nerves in the small of the back ache. The shoulders and arms give no more pain but there is a slight latent irritation on the skin which from time to time prickles. I have also a very strange feeling of pins and needles but I think it is going off."

When a course of treatment has once been prescribed Mr. Churchill obeys his doctor's instructions faithfully but otherwise dismisses the matter from his mind.

Mr. Churchill has a profound respect for the medical profession. You must be fit in body and mind to get the most out of living, he once said to me. And to the men who repair the machine when some part of it gets out of order he is sincerely grateful. I was struck, for instance, by the fact that, whereas so many of the acquaintances he made in America were soon forgotten, Mr. Churchill has always remained on the most cordial terms with Dr. Otto Pickhardt, the New York specialist who attended him when he was knocked down by an automobile on Fifth Avenue three days after landing in the United States. When Mr. Churchill heard that Dr. Pickhardt was coming to England he cabled him an invitation to be his guest at Chartwell and later received him with great cordiality. For many years the two men have corresponded regularly.

Unless Mr. Churchill is actually sick, which is very seldom, he does not worry about his health and accepts his expanding girth with contented resignation. I have never seen him on a slimming diet.

A man who has led a life as full and well rounded as Mr. Churchill can afford to view the long years behind him with philosophic detachment. Mr. Churchill has always lived intensely in the present; he has derived from the passing moment every ounce of enjoyment and excitement that it had to offer. Today his attitude toward life remains unchanged. In spirit he is as young as when the *Daily Mail* dubbed him "The Youngest Man in Europe" and that was forty years ago.

*Chapter VIII*

# HIS WORDS HAVE WINGS

❖

THOUGH I HAVE OFTEN listened to his speeches in the making, I, too, have been impressed by the magnificent way in which Mr. Churchill has eloquently and movingly told the world the story of Britain's heroic war effort. No one who has listened to these speeches on the radio or read them in the newspapers can fail to realize that here is one of the greatest English orators of all time. What most people do not realize is the "blood, sweat, and toil" that have made Mr. Churchill the incomparable organist of the English language that he is today.

Winston Churchill was born and grew up with a stutter and a defect in his palate that caused him to lisp. You could ask for no more impressive tribute to the man's perseverance than the fact that he has never allowed this staggering handicap to deflect him one inch from the path he chose to tread. There are few men with a speech defect who would even think of embarking upon a political career.

Mr. Churchill has never fully cured the lisp. I found it very pronounced all the time I took dictation from him. And the stutter still breaks out violently whenever he is excited—which is often. But on the public platform and before the microphone there is no stutter and the lisp is imperceptible. Even I, who know it exists, cannot detect it, for there a miracle of will power somehow triumphs over Nature's limitations.

Mr. Churchill has accomplished this miracle by hard work and that quality in his makeup which exults in meeting difficulties and mastering them. On the platform, I have observed, he gets around the defects in his speech by launching his words in small phrases and in a curious staccato tempo. His sentences seem to tumble in measured periods from his lips.

I have heard Mr. Churchill himself confess

that in his younger days he had a weakness for the "purple patch." I once saw him laughingly call to the attention of one of his publishers a phrase he had written at the time when he took pride in being the *enfant terrible* of the Conservative Party. He had described war as "a world of monstrous shadows moving in convulsive combinations through vistas of fathomless catastrophe." He excused this by saying "that's what comes of reading too much Gibbon."

Today you can see—and I doubt whether he would be as willing to confess to this—that he still loves a grandiose touch. He has spoken on occasion of "a cataract of disaster" and of "the long night of barbarism unbroken by the star of hope."

Yet Mr. Churchill's speech is not somber, his language is not that of tragedy. It is simple in the main, often witty, at times frivolous, a magnificent fusion of contradictory elements. And when you least expect it the roguish schoolboy in him bubbles irrepressibly to the surface, a fact that members of the House find rather disconcerting.

Mr. Churchill has built his oratory on the surest of all foundations, a superb command of the

English language. How he acquired it is a question that, I noticed, enormously intrigues all of his new acquaintances. And sooner or later they never fail to ask him about it. It is a curious story and one that Mr. Churchill loves to tell himself.

"At thirteen," he enjoys reminding his hearers, "I passed into the bottom of the bottom form of Harrow and remained there for a year. This gave me a splendid advantage over the brighter boys. You see, while the others were learning Latin and Greek we dunces were taught only English. So I really got a good grasp of English construction, which is a very fine thing to know."

In his later years at Harrow, Mr. Churchill recalls, he "shone" at English and composition but remained woefully ill-read. Two years devoted to the study of strategy and military history at Sandhurst did nothing to fill this gap in his education. But when he was 21, his regiment was dispatched to India and while his fellow officers were enjoying their long afternoon siesta, Lieutenant Churchill began his literary apprenticeship. He wrote to his mother in England for books on history, philosophy, and economics. And for the next two years he read them voraciously.

Mr. Churchill recalls starting with the Bible, Darwin and Malthus. He studied carefully the prose of Gibbon and Macaulay and was strongly under their influence when he first started to write. Macaulay especially became his literary model and, he admits with a smile, his hero. I once came across a little biography of Mr. Churchill in a copy of the London *Daily Mail*. It was dated back to 1900 or thereabouts. The author titled his sketch, "The Youngest Man in Europe," and in it I found this remark, "At dinner he talks and talks and you can never tell when he leaves off quoting his one idol, Macaulay, and begins with the other, Winston Churchill."

Mr. Churchill has often said he was glad he educated himself in the days when learning had not yet been "canned" for easy consumption. He believes that everyone should read the great authors and thinkers in the original text and learn to become their own critic and commentator. "It's an exercise that makes you do some hard thinking and that's very good for all of us."

Churchill's reading tastes might be considered

highbrow. History and biography are his favorite subjects. Military strategy comes next. He glances through any books on politics or economics that have created a stir. His favorite English poet is A. E. Housman. He prefaced the first volume of his *World Crisis* with these lines from *The Shropshire Lad:*

> "On the idle hills of summer
>   Sleepy with the flow of streams
> Far I hear the steady drummer
>   Drumming like a noise in dreams.
>
> Far and near, and low and louder
>   On the roads of earth go by
> Dear to friends, and food for powder
>   Soldiers marching, all to die."

Light reading does not interest Mr. Churchill greatly for the simple reason that he finds no need to "relax." His serious reading, his articles and his hobbies are relaxation enough.

When once he had acquired the reading habit, Mr. Churchill never again lost it. In his first bachelor apartment in Mayfair, I was told by a friend of his, the books overflowed the study, the living room and the bedroom—and shelves had to be constructed in the bathroom. At Chartwell Manor in Kent, Mr. Churchill has a magnificent library and when he travels he takes quantities of books with him and amasses others *en route*. Wherever he is sitting, there is a pile of books at his elbow; his bed is always littered with them. And he reads voraciously far into the night, however exhausting the day's work may have been. Incidentally, his favorite gift to people is an autographed, leather-bound copy of one of his own works.

People sometimes ask Mr. Churchill whether he makes notes on his reading or tries to memorize the best passages. He used to do it, he admits, when he was forming a style and preparing himself for the future. When I worked with him, however, I did not see him do much of this. He has—I think I have said this already, but it is worth repeating—a perfectly phenomenal memory. Nowadays he can carry most of his notes in his head and I shouldn't think they ever get mislaid there.

The creating of a Churchillian speech or arti-

cle is a remarkable process. I have taken part in
it many times with my pad and pencil, and have
never failed to be infected by Mr. Churchill's
enthusiasm. It struck me that his behavior was
rather like that of an explorer who has to plan
an expedition over uncharted territory. At first
he literally doesn't know how he is going to reach
his destination. But very soon he gets his bearings
and before long has hit upon the right track.
When that happens he seems to experience the
thrill of having made an exciting discovery, and
he communicates it to everyone around him.

I can see him now, pacing slowly up and down
the room, his hands clasped behind his back, his
shoulders hunched, his head sunk forward in deep
thought, slowly and haltingly dictating the beginning of a speech or an article. . . . I wait, my
pencil poised in midair, as he whispers phrases to
himself, carefully weighing each word and striv-
ing to make his thoughts balance. Nothing may
be put down until it has been tested aloud and
found satisfactory. A happy choice brings a glint
of triumph to his eye; a poor one is instantly
discarded. He will continue the search until every
detail—of sound, rhythm and harmony—is to his

liking. Sometimes there are long halts, during which he patiently sounds out a phrase a dozen times, this way and that, making the cigar in his hand serve as a baton to punctuate the rhythm of his words.

After a period of painful groping a change comes over him. I remember his saying once in a letter to Mr. Chenery, the editor of *Collier's Magazine,* in connection with the plan of some article he was preparing for him: "The mere fact of writing you this letter has made it all clear to me. *It has lit up my mind."*

That is actually what happens. And if you're working with him you really see the dawn break and share his sudden feeling of triumph. He becomes totally oblivious to everything around him. I'm sure that if I had got up and left the room he would have gone on dictating without noticing my absence.

From now on words flow easily, too easily for his secretary's liking. My pencil used to fly over the page in a desperate effort to keep up with him. He seldom hesitated or faltered.

It is a delight to watch him when he has swung into his stride. His face—that round, red, rather cupid face—shows that he is enjoying every moment of the game. It made me feel very conscious of a certain boylike quality in Mr. Churchill; his expression after he had overcome the first difficulties of a speech and laid down the main lines of his exposition reminded me of a youth wrapt in happy concentration after unraveling the workings of some complicated mechanical toy.

I was amazed to discover one day that Mr. Churchill had more or less worked out the whole method of preparing a speech some forty years ago, before he had made one single public utterance. Being naturally very interested in his literary career, I dropped into the library of the British Museum one free afternoon to find out exactly how many books he had written in his busy life and what they were about. Running down the title index, my eye came upon *Savrola—a Tale*. I did not suspect that Mr. Churchill had written any novels at all, and curiosity prompted me to take a look at what I correctly guessed to have been a youthful effort. The story was about "Savrola," leader of the Democratic Party in the mythical state of Laurania, a man "vehement and of a high daring cast of mind." It was obviously a romantic self-portrait of young Mr. Churchill. What particularly struck me was one passage in which the author describes Savrola's method of preparing a speech: "Amid the smoke he saw his peroration—a fine thought and a fine simile expressed in that diction which is comprehensible even to the most illiterate, appeals even to the simplest. His ideas began to group themselves into sentences; he murmured to himself; the rhythm of his style swayed him; instinctively he alliterated." But for the style it might be Britain's Prime Minister describing the way *he* prepares a speech today. And Mr. Churchill, like Savrola, still loves alliteration and is not afraid to use it: "We cannot fail or falter," "A man of light and learning," and so forth.

Mr. Churchill's speeches have often been compared—and rightly, I think—to a great symphony. In them thought and feeling seem to be perfectly blended in a magnificent orchestration. As I took them down I experienced something of the thrill you get from hearing a great piece of music for the first time.

I must confess to being one of the people for whom words have always held a fascination. Most

English schoolchildren are well grounded in the classics of their own literature; and I was no exception to the rule. The beauty and rhythm of the sentences that were taking shape on the pages of my notebook were quite unmistakable. If Mr. Churchill enjoyed himself, I certainly did too. It was exciting to work at the elbow of so fine a master of the English language and, so to speak, to "sit in" on his creative labors.

I was genuinely sorry when such dictation ended and I had to go off to transcribe my notes. As soon as I had finished them I took the typewritten pages into Mr. Churchill for revision. Fountain pen in hand, he would go over the manuscript two, three, sometimes as many as six times, deleting whatever seemed redundant or superfluous, adding a word or a phrase here and there in his delicate, flowing handwriting. Then I would take it away and make a clean copy. Generally the process had to be repeated at least once, sometimes three times or four, until the manuscript seemed to him as near perfect as possible.

Whenever Mr. Churchill has time he memorizes every word, every joke, every gesture of a speech. I understand that when he was younger he even used to rehearse before a mirror; but long experience has made that, at least, unnecessary. He likes his speeches typed on small pieces of notepaper with every line of each paragraph indented so that the first word catches his eye more easily.

As one might guess from all this, Mr. Churchill is not a good extemporaneous speaker. For many years before entering the House of Commons he would learn by heart and have typed out in full two or three and sometimes as many as six speeches, to be ready for any turn the debate might take. Nevertheless, Mr. Churchill has taught himself by years of patient practice to create the impression of spontaneity when he speaks. He is always in close touch with his audience and can rise magnificently to a difficult situation.

I witnessed an amazing demonstration of this when he was speaking before an audience of 20,000 in a huge building designed for sporting events and not at all appropriate for a lecture. In the middle of the speech the amplification system broke down without Mr. Churchill immediately noticing it, and naturally there were angry cries of "Louder! Louder!" In a few seconds the audience might have degenerated into a howling mob with which no speaker could have coped.

Mr. Churchill knew exactly what to do, and did it quickly. Advancing to the very edge of the platform, he raised his hands for quiet. Then, grasping the portable microphone which hung from his left lapel, he held it aloft for all to see; and with a dramatic gesture flung it onto the the ground where it smashed to pieces. Facing the crowd, he thundered in a fine, clear voice that all could hear, "Now that we have exhausted the resources of science we shall fall back upon Mother Nature and do our best!" And to his last word he held his audience spellbound. As he ended, the crowd roared: "Good old Winnie! You can't down him!"

On the lecture platform and in the House of Commons Mr. Churchill instinctively assumes a Napoleonic pose, his feet slightly apart, his short, stocky body rocking on his heels, his two hands grasping the lapels of his coat. As he speaks he throws his head slightly back and the sonorous sentences, once projected from his lips, seem to be carried to the farthest corners of the hall by their own momentum.

His reputation as a phrasemaker is unmatchable and unmatched. A score or more of his utterances have in a few brief months become common coin among English-speaking people: "Blood and toil, tears and sweat," "Never in the field of human conflict was so much owed by so many to so few," "Let us to the task, to the battle and the toil," "This was their finest hour," "Give us the tools and we will finish the job." It is the sort of language that a nation at war likes to hear.

Mr. Churchill has made several lecture tours in this country and I was with him on one of them. His behavior on that occasion showed me an entirely different side of the man and a side of him that most people have not had occasion to notice.

Doing the lecture circuit may seem an easy way of earning a great deal of money—to those who have never done it. It isn't. It means spending every other night on the train. It means getting up at Kalamazoo, Michigan, at the crack of dawn because the only train from your previous stop reaches Kalamazoo, Michigan, at the crack of dawn. It means revising speeches in taxicabs and dressing out of suitcases. It means always being the social lion for the local lion hunters, however tired and out-of-sorts one may feel. It means eating caterers' meals. It means living by a train schedule. (For a lecturer there are two unforgivable sins: to arrive without a speech and not to arrive at all; and the second is much worse.) But all of these Mr. Churchill accepted almost cheerfully.

From the start of his tour he regarded himself as his lecture manager's employee, and being a man who expects complete satisfaction from those he employs, he was bent on giving complete satisfaction himself. However early or however late he had to catch a train to make his next engagement he acquiesced as a matter of course. Stricken down with acute laryngitis at Toledo, Ohio, he insisted on going through with his lecture in defiance of doctors' orders and spent the whole day gargling, spraying his throat, sucking lozenges, taking large doses of medicine, waging a savage blitzkrieg against the affliction that might stop him from doing his duty by his lecture manager. And, of course, he made a splendid speech. He is always at his best when fighting something.

Mr. Churchill knew that his lecture manager had gambled heavily on his drawing power. He had received the highest fee ever paid to any lecturer at any time in any country. Consequently it became a point of honor to prove his worth and prove it he did. His audiences varied from 3000 to 8000, which is not far from a record.

I myself always thought it rather strange that people flocked so eagerly to these lectures. They were devoid of the flashes of humor, the terrific punch and the majestic overtones that characterize Mr. Churchill's orations in the House of Commons.

He spoke on three subjects: "The Destiny of the English Speaking Peoples," "The War Debts," and "The Problem of Gold" and generally talked above the heads of his audience. It is characteristic, however, that he never made the same speech twice. After each engagement he would think of a number of improvements and would set to work the next morning on the text of his address. He polished and repolished his speeches endlessly so that they seemed to grow continuously in scope and depth. And there, incidentally, you have one of the keys to Churchill the man. Like his speeches he never stops growing.

Mr. George Jean Nathan once said to me that writing was at first like turning on a tap that hasn't been used for a long time. The water begins by running thick and cloudy, in spurts and gushes; then, after a while, it comes out clear and flows freely.

Winston Churchill more than any writer I have known—and I have known a number, would-be and professional, in my lifetime—has the ability to tap the reservoir of creative effort that in most people lies unused. Most writers seem to experience the most fantastic difficulty in getting started. They will talk endlessly about the books they have written or the books they are going to write, about agents, reviewers, rival authors, publishers, anything to put off the awful moment when they have nothing to do but sit down and write. They generally call it "waiting for inspiration." Mr. Churchill is a model they could all profitably imitate. Years ago he taught himself not to consult his feelings or to go sighing for "inspiration" but to make his inspiration an obedient servant, responsive to his master's call.

When a job of writing has to be done Mr. Churchill sits down to it whether he is in the mood or not and the effort generates his creative power. He always works under great pressure and seems to enjoy it genuinely.

At Chartwell Manor, in Kent, there is a long room on the first floor where Mr. Churchill does all his writing, or rather his dictation, since he never writes or types anything himself. One side of the room is entirely given up to a very long table on which are kept many reference books. His secretary sits at the head of the table taking dictation. He has a male secretary and research expert present also. Whenever he isn't quite sure of a fact he turns to him for information. As he dictates he walks up and down the room lost in deep concentration.

His historical data are always collected and checked by a group of experts. When he was writing his life of his ancestor, the Duke of Marlborough, he called in a naval and a military expert to gather data for him on the specialized aspects of that famous soldier's career. When all these aides have collected the material he needs for a book he studies it carefully, absorbs it thoroughly and then writes the whole book straight off from memory.

I am told that he is never late in delivering his manuscript to his publishers. When a manuscript goes to press he has six sets of galleys made and sends them to different sets of experts to be checked. He has a mania for accuracy and one will be hard put to detect errors of fact in any of his works.

It is as a writer that Churchill has earned his living. His father left him with a taste for the best of everything and only a small fortune with which to gratify it. Fortunately his books, though he has seldom written on popular subjects, have sold amazingly well, well enough to have brought him in, together with his journalistic earnings, an income of about $100,000 a year. His *The World Crisis* netted him $100,000; his biography of his father, Lord Randolph Churchill, though it only just broke even in the United States, earned for him eight thousand pounds from the English sales.

The advance payments made to Mr. Churchill have been among the largest in publishing history for the type of book he writes. He has always been hard up and any publisher who wanted a book from him had to be generous in the matter of advances. He does not haggle about money matters but knows exactly how much he wants and generally gets it without argument.

One of his American publishers, who has been associated with Mr. Churchill for over twenty years, told me that he advanced $16,000 for *The World Crisis*—a history of the First World War— and still he made a slight profit on it. Mr. Churchill, he said, had planned to call it "The Great Amphibian" because the scene of the book was laid on sea as well as on land. He and his associates had objected, and finally Mr. Churchill had agreed to the title *The World Crisis*. This book, which was to have been a two volume work finally spread itself over four volumes.

On his life of the Duke of Marlborough, Mr. Churchill's American publisher made one of the greatest advances in the history of his firm. *A*

*Roving Commission*—the record of Mr. Churchill's early years—published in 1930, was his most
popular book from the point of view of American
sales. A condensation of it appeared again ten
years later in the *Reader's Digest*. Here again Mr.
Churchill deferred to his publishers' judgment
regarding the title. He himself had wanted to
call it "Thoughts and Adventures."

Mr. Churchill's latest work, his as yet unpub-
lished *History of the English-Speaking Peoples*,
has already made publishing history. An English
firm, Cassells, paid him a lump sum of $100,000
for it, the largest down payment of its kind ever
made in England. They bought all rights to the
manuscript and promptly insured Mr. Churchill's
life for a corresponding sum.

The idea for this book really originated in a
suggestion made to Mr. Churchill as far back as
1929 by a friend in New York who asked him if
he had ever thought of writing the story of the
development of the British Empire. The idea
immediately appealed to him immensely. In 1931,
when he was again in this country, he went to
see his friend about it. I must thank this gentle-

man, who prefers to remain anonymous, for an amusing record of that interview.

"Churchill behaved as though he had come to discuss a conspiracy," he told me. "He shut the door and sat down beside me at the desk. His manner was very dramatic. He wasted no time in getting to the point of his visit. 'That was a wonderful idea of yours,' he said, as though I had made the suggestion the day before and had it still fresh in my mind. 'But I think I've improved on it. I'm going to write a history of the English-speaking peoples. What do you think of that!' He beamed triumphantly and waited for my reaction to this bombshell. I agreed it was an epochal idea and that seemed to please him."

All of Mr. Churchill's books were financially successful in the United States except his four-volume life of Marlborough. It was purely historical and had no popular appeal. Although it was originally intended to run to only 200,000 words it eventually exceeded 1,000,000.

Mr. Churchill is passionately interested in history. England, of course, has always been his special field but he is also an expert on the American

Civil War; and a large section of his library at Chartwell is devoted to works on Napoleon.

Mr. Churchill's mind is always teeming with ideas for books. He used to say humorously: "I shall never live long enough to write all the books I have in mind."

No one man possibly could.

Though Mr. Churchill is the author of twenty-two full-sized volumes, he has at the same time been a very prolific journalist. He has always been ready and willing to write for newspapers and magazines if called upon by an editor, and quite often he would approach them with suggestions himself. But the big-paying markets are the only ones that interest him.

When Mr. Churchill was in America several editors of the so-called "quality" magazines approached him for articles. They were astonished and not a little disconcerted, I am afraid, to discover that he would write nothing for less than $1000, and expected $1500 for a full-length article. He has a very keen sense of his own commercial value. And there were plenty of magazines only too pleased to pay his price.

Most editors have found him easy to work with. Several American editors to whom I have talked were particularly impressed by his willingness to accept their point of view and bow to their superior knowledge of the American market. He admitted to them freely that he didn't understand the reading habits of this country. His ideas, as a rule, were too historical or, at any rate, too much on the highbrow side. But he was always willing to modify his treatment until exactly the right "slant" had been achieved.

A good example was a piece on the idea of monarchy which he wrote for Mr. Chenery of *Collier's Magazine*. The article was, of course, too abstract for the general reader. After consultation with Mr. Chenery Mr. Churchill changed it to a portrait of King Alfonso of Spain. It was still not quite satisfactory. He again set to work to recast it and did this three or four times, much to the concern of his agent who considered *Collier's* requirements rather exacting.

When Mr. Churchill saw Mr. Chenery a few days after the final draft had been approved, he asked him: "Was that final rewrite satisfactory?"

Mr. Chenery assured him "it was a grand job."

"Don't ever hesitate to be frank with me," said Mr. Churchill, "I'm a professional journalist and I'm always willing to cooperate."

He proved this in more ways than one. He always tried to write exactly as many words as were wanted. But he raised no objections to having his manuscripts cut, if necessary, and was content to leave the titles to his editors' judgment. For a long period *Collier's* had a running contract with him for six to eight articles a year at top prices. Incidentally, Mr. Churchill shares with Mr. Lloyd George the distinction of having been among the highest paid journalists in the world.

Though Mr. Churchill has a healthy flair for a sensational story he will never write one unless he feels the facts completely justify it. In the summer of 1939, Mr. Chenery called him at Chartwell by transatlantic telephone to ask if he would write an article saying there would be no war.

"Certainly not," Mr. Churchill replied.

Mr. Chenery then asked: "Will you write us an article saying there *will* be a war?"

"Certainly not," said the voice from England. "But I will write an article estimating the forces making for war and the forces making for peace."

And then and there, in a fifteen minute conversation across the Atlantic, he outlined the main lines of what proved to be a very successful article, which he delivered in record time to meet an early deadline.

Mr. Churchill likes to discuss his books and articles over lunch or dinner and most of the editors and publishers with whom he has worked have become his very good friends. They were experts in their field and Mr. Churchill has a great respect for experts. He would ask them searching questions about the American market.

*Chapter IX*

# HIS FAITH IS INSPIRING

❖

My personal opinion is that the solid foundation of Mr. Churchill's prodigious achievements is his boundless zest for living, his keen sense of personal integrity and an infinite capacity for taking pains.

At the British Embassy in Paris I frequently heard people remark, a trifle superciliously, that Mr. Churchill was "brilliant but erratic." I realized after working with him a very short time that he had disciplined this "brilliant but erratic" mind until its tidiness could have served as a model for every civil servant. His meticulous personal attention to detail was a constant source of astonishment to me.

Few men have been born with the inexhaustible vitality of Mr. Churchill. He always made me

think of a volcano in eruption. But Mr. Churchill, forewarned perhaps by the tragic end of his
father who died quite worn out at the age of 46,
has taught himself to guard his health and con-
serve his restless energy. Today in his loping
stride and buoyant manner and in those fearless
blue eyes you still see the mark of youth. Mr.
Churchill at 66 is cheerfully shouldering a task
that would appall a man half his years.

Mr. Churchill's honesty is one of his outstanding qualities. Time and again I have seen him
refuse gifts in order to be under no obligation,
real or imaginary, to any man. Sergeant Thompson told me that the day he became Chancellor
of the Exchequer he sold every stock in his pos-
session. When he was Air Minister and he had an
Air Force car at his disposal, he kept a strict record of the mileage run on his own private business
and paid for all the gas thus consumed.

This is one side of the man I knew—hard
worker, wise liver and scrupulously honest ad-
ministrator.

Then there is the side that Sir Ernest Moir told

me about years before I went to work for Mr. Churchill: "There's a lot of the Yankee in Winston. He knows how to hustle and how to make others hustle too."

It can be called "hustling" or "prodding," there's something in Mr. Churchill that is always on the lookout for new and more efficient ways of getting things done. He has no use for conventions that have outlived their usefulness and he sets to work on official red tape with a large and ruthless pair of shears.

It was at his express command that the British Civil Service took the revolutionary step of substituting "Yes" for "The answer is in the affirmative" in its official communications. While directing the war against the Nazis he has found time to wage a stern campaign at home against the absurdity of the outdated "officialese" that had become the language of English bureaucracy. He has been responsible for removing to a large extent the deadweight of muddling, hesitancy and downright incompetence from English life. He has set the wheels of Britain's war effort turning at top speed and has galvanized his countrymen into action. He has "prodded" every man, woman and child into making a call on their inner strength, into giving forth an extra effort, that has turned a nation of leisurely, phlegmatic, peace-loving people into an army of indomitable fighters.

"Go To It!" is England's wartime slogan. I think it has unconsciously been the guiding maxim of Mr. Churchill's life.

But again there lurks within the recesses of this kaleidoscopic character an irrepressible, irresponsible small boy who delights in colored bathroom fixtures, visits to the theatre with Mary, his youngest daughter, and singing songs with Diana his eldest; a small boy who was so enchanted with the first record of a speech of his made by the British Broadcasting Company that in his haste to play it over on his gramophone he broke it and was utterly disconsolate until a second record was made. Even in these grim times you see this gay buoyancy popping to the surface. I can't help feeling that the schoolboy in Mr. Churchill secretly delights in flaunting Hitler with his jauntily poised cigar, his bulldog manner and his amazing array of hats.

All these different personalities of the man combine to make Mr. Churchill a great world figure, the product of an immense vitality, harnessed to a powerful intellect and directed by an iron will. But they do not explain his genius.

It is doubtful, I suppose, whether genius can ever be completely explained. But again and again I have asked myself the question: What is it that makes Mr. Churchill seem to tower above the most brilliant of his contemporaries? And I think I have found the answer.

It is impossible to work with Mr. Churchill for any length of time and not sense that he feels upon himself the hand of Destiny. Even when English politics were dominated by a group of statesmen all of whom had completely repudiated Winston Churchill, everyone around him took it for granted that these years were only an interlude in his life; that some day when the English people had grown tired of mediocrities Winston Churchill's qualities would carry him to the premiership. How many times I have heard his friends say: "When Winston is Prime Minister . . ." And the odd thing is that very soon I found myself accepting this idea as perfectly natural and inevitable.

Mr. Churchill himself once told one of his intimates that he was taking advantage of this "temporary" absence from office "to put my house and my life in order." There was obviously no doubt in his mind that this period in his life was a prelude to the playing of his greatest role.

This faith in his destiny is happily linked to an infallible flair for the "right," even though it might be a spectacular gesture. Mr. Churchill was born with an intuitive sense of the dramatic. I cannot help feeling that he has always seen himself as a leading figure in the drama of history.

When he turned to politics and journalism the English stage lost a great actor. But on the stage of English politics Mr. Churchill has managed by the force and power of his personality to monopolize much of the spotlight. His chimney-pot hats, his inevitable cigar and the lavender shelter suit he is said to wear in London today—are not these unconscious idiosyncrasies of the born actor who senses what his public enjoys and lets them have it?

I came to the conclusion that there was an element of mysticism in Mr. Churchill's implicit faith in his mission. He is not religious in the sense that a man like Lord Halifax is; he has no natural faith, no instinctive piety. Rather his own successes induce in him a feeling of awe, of reverence and gratitude toward the Providence that has treated him so kindly and guarded him so well.

He seems to have a simple, rather typically English belief in God—The God of Rudyard Kipling, the Empire Builders and the country squire. He knows his Bible well and quotes it frequently. But his choice of quotations is characteristic: "Ask, and it shall be given you, . . . knock, and it shall be opened unto you: . . ." He quotes a God who helps those who help themselves.

Along with this faith in himself and Providence goes an almost uncanny prophetic insight and a unique breadth and originality of vision. So far as I could judge Mr. Churchill has never been influenced by the mob mind. Rather he has consistently prejudiced his own career by standing uncompromisingly for his principles in the face of public sentiment.

He has never been afraid to hold extreme views and to express them without regard for the consequences. In his early days this scion of the Marlboroughs dared to advocate, in forthright language, a New Deal for England: "We want a Government that will think a little more about the toiler at the bottom of the mine and a little less about fluctuations of the stock market in London. We want a government and a policy that will think the condition of a slum in an English city is not less worthy of the attention of statesmen and of Parliament than the jungle of Somaliland."

Though an aristocrat and a Conservative at heart, as head of the Board of Trade he introduced the eight-hour day in the mines and was instrumental in the institution of Labor Exchanges and Trade Boards to regulate wages. Though an imperialist and even a jingoist, he counselled a moderate peace after the Boer War, was in favor of giving the Irish Home Rule and wished to lift the food blockade against Germany after the Armistice.

He has always done his best to live up to his political credo: "In war, Resolution; in defeat, Defiance; in victory, Magnanimity."

Mr. Churchill's prophetic insight, that made him realize long before his contemporaries the crucial role of the plane and the tank in modern war, has been strikingly demonstrated in the last seven years. He was one of the few British statesmen to recognize as far back as 1933 that the rise of Hitlerism must inevitably lead to a second and more terrible conflict. And he lost no opportunity of warning his countrymen.

But it is a thankless task to be a prophet. I was in London on the memorable 28th of September, 1938, when Churchill stood alone against the general desire for peace at all costs and I realized what a severe trial of strength he endured that day.

A dense grim-faced crowd was waiting anxiously outside of the Houses of Parliament. Neville Chamberlain was to make a momentous report to the nation on the failure of all efforts to find a peaceful solution to the Czech crisis and prepare England for war.

As the Prime Minister's car swept into the courtyard the anxious crowd cheered lustily. Then came a long black limousine in which Queen Mary sat bolt upright as usual. The crowd raised its cheer louder. But the anxious faces did not brighten.

Later, in the House, Mr. Chamberlain was describing his "last effort" to avert war when a message arrived from Herr Hitler inviting him to a four-power conference at Munich the next day. The Prime Minister's announcement that he would leave at once for Munich was greeted with a terrific burst of cheering. The members of Parliament, irrespective of party, clapped each other on the back, leaped up on their seats and made the ancient rafters of the House of Commons ring with their cheers. The Archbishop of Canterbury came forward to offer Mr. Chamberlain his hearty congratulations. The House was with him almost to a man. Almost, but not quite.

Mr. Churchill came out into Palace Yard with his face as black as a thundercloud, his cigar clamped ferociously between his teeth. In a few hours the whole country knew that he stood firm against appeasement. The evening papers scornfully called him "an alarmist," a "Tory Cassandra" and lightly discarded his prophecies of disaster.

But I was leaving for America in a few days and derived no comfort from the Munich Settlement. It was to me a gloomy departure, saddened by a premonition that I was seeing the last of the England in which I had grown up.

At home in Suffolk there was none of the hysterical rejoicing with which Londoners had greeted the Munich Agreement. My brother was continuing grimly with the work of distributing gas masks to his parishioners. Even my mother, an irrepressible optimist, shook her head sadly as she read her morning newspaper. And I remember the little maid who helped me pack asking anxiously, "When do you think it will come, Miss?" England was resigned, dispirited, rather like a patient awaiting a dreaded operation.

I visited Virginia Woolf and her husband the day before sailing. They too were convinced that Munich was only a reprieve which at best would provide a breathing space in which to prepare for the terrible conflict ahead. In the drawing room of Mrs. Woolf's lovely house in Tavistock Square, in which the soft-colored chintzes and the modern English paintings formed a background so expressive of the refinement and distinction of the most civilized influences in English life, we sipped tea and talked grimly of the horrors of the next war. It would mean, Virginia Woolf said, the descent of a total intellectual night over Europe. The war would last many years and our generation would see much that it held dear destroyed. We talked of the possibility of new leaders. Mrs. Woolf reminded me that England's greatest strength was her ability to produce a leader when one was needed. In the last war it had been Lloyd George. Now there were Winston Churchill and Anthony Eden and the Labor leaders.

Well, England did produce a leader. Mr. Churchill was assigned to the role he had so long waited for—but only when the whole stage threatened to collapse under him at any moment. And yet, just two months after he had shouldered his predecessor's legacy of defeat, a young British soldier wrote these words to a friend in America: "England, at last, is a real nation, really led; a handful of able, brave, resolute men, and one genuinely great man at the top. The whole rhythm of our national life has changed. We think virilely; we hold ourselves as men who know what we must face and what we must do. We are alive again. There is a meaning in poetry and sacrifice and young men going to die, and the sudden glory of a few snatched hours of leave and love."

How did Mr. Churchill dispel the doubts, the fears, the hesitations, and infuse his countrymen with the spirit that is today the wonder of the supporters of Democracy the world over? I think he did it largely by his own unquestioning faith in the greatness of ordinary men. I have heard him state that men can rise to any ordeal, endure untold suffering, endless hardship, even death, if they believe wholeheartedly in their cause. The idea of death and hardship does not dismay Mr. Churchill.

After he himself had once been at death's door he wrote these very revealing words: "Nature is merciful and does not try her children, man or beast, beyond their compass. Live dangerously, dread naught, and all will be well."

I never detected an ounce of sentimentality in the man, and that perhaps is what makes him one of the greatest war leaders of all time. When death and danger come all must share it. He was opposed to evacuating British children to the Western Hemisphere because shipping space was scarce. He was thus delighted to read one day last summer in the London *Times* a letter written by a boy of eleven to his father that completely reflected his own feelings toward this acute controversy.

"I am writing to beg you not to let me go to Canada (I suppose you know that we are probably going)," the little boy was quoted, "a. Because I don't want to leave England in time of war. Prejudice apart, if it had been peacetime I should have opened my mind to it. b. Because I should be very homesick; I am feeling likewise now. c. Because it would be kinder to let me be killed with you, if such happened (which is quite unlikely) than to allow me to drift to strangers and finish my happy childhood in a contrary fashion. d. I would not see you for an indefinite time, perhaps never again. Letters would simply redouble my homesickness.

"These are my reasons and I hope that you can take them into consideration. I can't do anything myself but I implore you to reason. I am not asking to live in London; I am merely asking not to leave the country.

"P.S. I would rather be bombed in fragments than leave England."

The letter was signed "X."

Mr. Churchill was apparently enormously pleased with it. It summed up exactly the point of view that he had been trying to convey to the nation. It was not a painful duty but a glorious privilege to share England's danger in this, "her finest hour." And a boy of eleven had mirrored his feelings and had expressed it with such simple eloquence!

Right away Mr. Churchill set his secretary to find out the name of the child. Calls were put through to the *Times* and very soon the writer was disclosed to be the son of Mr. Wedgewood Benn, a member of Parliament. Immediately Mr. Churchill—at that moment probably the busiest man in the world—sat down and wrote to the boy, telling him that he had read his letter, thoroughly approved of his attitude and was sending him an autographed copy of one of his books.

Mr. Churchill has said that he would make any sacrifice if he thought it would bring his country one step nearer to victory. He has said that he would have England fight "on the beaches, on the landing grounds, in the fields, in the streets, in the hills" rather than surrender. In an ordinary man one would call it inhumanity. In a war leader it is the quality that kindles the fighting spirit of a nation.

As a war leader, Mr. Churchill has at last found his mission. His qualities that I learned so well at first hand and the defects of his qualities fit him preeminently for the task that has now fallen to him. All of his personal ambitions are swallowed up in the one selfless determination to bring England through. "Over-engined" I have heard someone call him. He is "over-engined" for peace perhaps but perfectly engined, I think, for war. For the first time in his life probably he has found a task that engages all of his energies, that calls forth all of the greatness in him.

It is a struggle after his own heart. Destiny has honored him with a supreme responsibility; the future of Democracy is in his keeping. I cannot help feeling that all of his life he has been preparing himself for some such role. And when it was thrust upon him he was ready for it. He knew what to do and he did it. And he knew what to say to the world.

"You ask what is our policy? I say it is to wage war by land, sea, and air—war with all our might and all the strength God has given us—and to wage war against a monstrous tyranny never surpassed in the dark and lamentable catalogues of human crime. That is our policy.

"You ask what is our aim? I can answer in one word. It is Victory. Victory at all costs. Victory in spite of all terrors. Victory, however long and hard the road may be, for without victory there is no survival."

And later: "We shall not fail or falter; we shall not weaken or tire. Neither the sudden shock of battle nor the long-drawn trials of vigilance and exertion will wear us down."

Never in the field of human conflict was so much owed by so many to this one man—WINSTON CHURCHILL.

# HIGHLIGHTS OF HIS LIFE

❖

THE BAND PLAYED "See The Conquering Hero Comes" as a handsome young man with red hair and prominent blue eyes mounted the platform to address the constituents of Oldham. When the music stopped, the mill girls took up the ditty that was sweeping England:

> You've heard of Winston Churchill;
> This is all I need to say—
> He's the latest and the greatest
> Correspondent of the day.

The young man began to speak and the crowd in this tough Lancashire factory town listened respectfully. Only a year before this scion of the Marlboroughs had presumed to stand as a "Tory Democrat" before the workers of the North to contest a by-election in the same city of Oldham. He had been rewarded with what he termed "a black eye."

But in a year he had achieved great things. Now he no longer came to plead for votes but to accept them. The citizens of Oldham were proud of his loyalty to them. He was England's idol. His spectacular exploits in the Boer War capped by a journalistic scoop had made him the most famous young man in Europe.

"At the rate he goes," the *Daily Mail* had said admiringly, "there will hardly be room for him in Parliament at thirty or in England at forty." At any rate, the constituents of Oldham thought that in the year 1900 Parliament needed him. They returned him by a large majority. Thus Winston Churchill was launched on a political career that was to carry him into nine Cabinet offices and raise him to the Premiership of England in "her finest hour."

But Mr. Churchill has really had three careers. He has been a newspaperman and a soldier and in politics. He has served as an officer in nine different regiments of the British Army and has risen to the rank of colonel. He has been one of the highest paid journalists in the world and has edited a newspaper with the largest daily circulation of its time.

Mr. Churchill's three careers were for long inextricably intermingled; his successes in one carried him on to further successes in another. He was swept into Parliament on the tide of a journalistic triumph which in turn was made possible by the subaltern's uniform that took him into the firing line on India's Northwest Frontier, in Egypt and in South Africa. For the first thirty years of Mr. Churchill's life it was hard to tell which came first—fighting, writing or the desire to govern England.

Mr. Churchill began his life with soldiering. There are two versions why he entered the army. The first is that one day when he was playing with his toy soldiers his father asked him what he wished to be when he grew up. "I want to be a general," he is supposed to have answered; and thereafter it was taken for granted that he would some day don the Queen's uniform.

The second version is simply that at school he was not considered bright enough for the law, and since he showed no leanings toward the Church, was left with no choice but the army—the only remaining profession for a gentleman.

As a small boy Mr. Churchill was once described as "a very interesting being though thoroughly uppish." Uppish he certainly was, and unruly, headstrong and violent into the bargain. At his first preparatory school he was punished regularly and once in a fit of rage kicked his headmaster's hat to shreds. His dancing teacher considered him "the naughtiest small boy in the world." But already he gave promise of unusual talents.

At the age of eight he became editor and publisher of a paper characteristically entitled, *The Critic*. There was only one issue. In the same year he acquitted himself very creditably in a school performance of Colman's *Heir At Law*. He had no trouble about remembering his lines, was not in the least shy and showed a keen sense of the dramatic which, if somewhat exaggerated, enchanted his schoolfellows.

Mr. Churchill passed into Harrow two places from the bottom of the school. "These two disappeared almost immediately through illness," he says in his autobiography. That year his father was the dominating personality in English politics. Visitors used to wait on the school steps to see young Churchill march by, and he grew accustomed to hearing them exclaim: "Why, he's last one of all!"

Young Churchill's trouble at Harrow was that he hated Latin and Greek, French and mathematics. But the army examination did not call for these subjects and he passed into Sandhurst over the heads of his seniors.

Sandhurst was a fresh start—and he loved it. At the end of two years he graduated with honors, eighth out of one hundred fifty, and was duly received into the 4th Hussars with a Second Lieutenant's Commission.

Lieutenant Churchill promptly fell in love with the glittering cavalry parades, the ceremonious mess dinners and vintage port of the British army. He fell in love with soldiering, too, and pined for his first taste of the thrill of action. The year was 1895, and unbroken peace reigned over the length and breadth of the Empire. But the Spanish, Churchill learned, were faced with a rebellion in Cuba, and young Winston, by pulling strings— and there were plenty of strings the son of Lord

Randolph could pull—got himself attached to the Spanish army as British observer.

The trip, however, would cost money, more money than his slender allowance would allow him to spend. The Churchills had never been a rich family. So he applied to the *Daily Graphic,* for which his father had written in the old days, and was duly commissioned to send in five "letters" on the Cuban campaign. That was the beginning of a long series of double assignments with the pen and the pistol. From then on Winston Churchill's activities as a soldier and as a journalist were inextricably mixed up, to the great indignation of Lieutenant Churchill's superior officers.

He fought in India and wrote for the *Daily Telegraph* the "Story of the Malakand Field Force," which later published in book form became a best seller and established then and there Churchill's literary reputation. He served with Kitchener against the Dervishes in the Sudan and wrote the *River War*. He covered the Boer War for the *Morning Post* at $1250 a month, was captured, made a miraculous escape and finally entered Pretoria in triumph in the vanguard of the victorious British Army.

Churchill was a tired editor's dream of the perfect correspondent. He didn't just write news, he made it. The combination produced a series of journalistic "scoops." Whenever a story broke, he was in the middle of it. By the time he had finished with it, it was no longer a story, it was a sensation. In the midst of the deadliest peril, his absolute sang-froid never deserted him. The story was the thing. Every detail, every sensation must be noted; every ounce of drama must be squeezed out of the occasion. "Keep cool, men," he enjoined his companions caught in an ambush during the Boer War. "This will make good copy for my paper."

It was during the Boer War, when it came to writing up his adventurous escape from the Boer prison camp, that young Churchill really excelled himself. That story "made" him. Every bit of drama, every element of suspense was extracted from the incident. Back in England people awaited with bated breath each instalment in the *Morning Post*. It was the journalistic sensation of the time. The "gigantic vulture" that had followed Winston Churchill across the veldt with its "hideous gurglings" became a national emblem and he became a national hero.

He has never forgotten that he owes a good measure of his political success to his journalistic prowess. Never a man to shun good publicity, he has been his own publicist. In office or out, his familiar by-line and the brilliant articles that go under it have done much to keep his personality in the forefront of English politics. It was as a "spot" reporter that Churchill did the most writing of his early days and his flair for "a story" has never deserted him.

Thirty years after the episode of the "gigantic vulture," Mr. Churchill was run over by an automobile on Fifth Avenue, in New York City. Again he was news. He had fifteen bones broken and suffered an internal hemorrhage; for two days his life was in danger. Naturally the public was hungry for details, and Churchill knew it. No sooner had he recovered from the first shock as he lay in his room in Lenox Hill Hospital than he began to write *My New York Misadventure*. He sold it to a syndicate for $2500. As before, his ability to think *and* feel in a moment of acute crisis produced a singular piece of reporting.

Apart from his schoolboy excursion into publishing with *The Critic,* Mr. Churchill has only been an editor once in his life. During the General Strike in 1926—he was Chancellor of the Exchequer at the time—he took over the *Morning Post,* whose ace war correspondent he had been a quarter of a century before, and put it out as the *British Gazette,* with spectacular success. He started with a circulation of 232,000. In three days he raised that circulation to 836,000. Five days later, when the strike ended and the *British Gazette* once again became the *Morning Post,* its circulation was 2,250,000, the largest in the world.

Winston Churchill, M.P.

Mr. Churchill was twenty-six when he entered Parliament. We have a striking portrait of him at this time, written for the *Daily Mail* by an American journalist, Julian Ralph: "Already Mr.

Churchill's head is carried with a droop which comes to those who read and study hard. When he is thinking he drops his head forward as if it were heavy. That is how you see him at one moment, a pose prophetic of what is too likely to fasten itself upon him before he reaches middle age. But it requires two plates to take a fair photograph of him, for the next time you look at him he has sprung to his feet with the eagerness of a boy, his pale blue eyes are sparkling, his lips are parted, he is talking a vocal torrent and hands and arms are driving home his words."

From the start of his Parliamentary career Mr. Churchill displayed those characteristics for which he later became famous. He showed a disconcerting lack of respect for "Party discipline." He insisted on doing his own thinking and there was a dangerous originality about his ideas that caused the Party big-wigs grave concern. What was infinitely worse than these heresies, he had an uncanny knack for focusing upon himself and his policies the attention of the public.

Mr. Churchill had entered Parliament as a Conservative; but he clung to his idea of "Tory Democracy" and based his program on the Radical slogan: "Peace, Retrenchment and Reform." When the subject of Protection became a Party issue he took the Liberal, anti-protectionist side and in a speech at Halifax thanked God "for the Liberal Party." That was too much. The Conservatives of Oldham met and passed a vote of no confidence in their member, the equivalent to expulsion from the Party.

Mr. Churchill was quite unperturbed. He simply crossed the House and took his seat among the members of the Liberal Party. The change was well timed. In the General Election of 1906, the Liberals won in a landslide. Nearly a quarter of a century of almost uninterrupted Conservative ascendancy was over. The Liberals were to enjoy power for a decade and Churchill was riding on the crest of their wave. In 1905 he became Under-Secretary for the Colonies in Campbell Bannerman's government. When "C.B." died suddenly in 1908 and Mr. Asquith took over the Premiership, he appointed Mr. Churchill President of the Board of Trade with a seat in the Cabinet.

## "The Fleet Was Ready"

In 1911, the increasingly tense situation in Europe took an ominous turn for the worse. All attempts to check the rearmament race had resulted in a deadlock. A crisis had flared over the dispatch of a German cruiser, the *Panther,* to Agadir in Morocco, then a French "zone of influence." The Balkan peoples were plotting to destroy the already dying Austro-Hungarian monarchy while Austria-Hungary was waiting for an excuse to swallow the rest of the Balkans and thus frustrate Russia's expansionist ambitions. This was the situation when Prime Minister Asquith invited Winston Churchill to play golf with him in Scotland and offered him the Admiralty on the 19th hole.

Needless to say Mr. Churchill jumped at the offer. He hurried to his desk under the portrait of Samuel Pepys, Father of the modern British Navy, and with a sublime disregard for convention, proceeded to make things hum in the Admiralty office in Whitehall. He looked for new blood, put the best men in the key positions, regardless of seniority, introduced the submarine and the 15-inch gun and fathered the British air arm.

In 1913, in a last effort to stave off the catastrophe that appeared to him inevitable, Mr. Churchill suggested to the Kaiser that both countries take a "naval holiday" that year. His statesman-like offer was contemptuously rejected and Mr. Churchill returned to the job of preparing the Fleet for war. That year he handed over to the "Invasion Committee" of the Cabinet a series of memoranda which he described as "imaginative exercises couched in a half-serious vein, designed to disturb complacency." The memoranda do not appear to have succeeded in this object.

When Churchill introduced the Naval Estimates—the largest in England's history—there was a terrific hubbub. But he literally stuck to his guns and by the autumn of that year he could face the future confident in the knowledge that his plans were well and carefully laid, and the Navy was ready.

Summer maneuvers for the year 1914 were fixed for July 14—the day that Austria drafted her ultimatum to Serbia. Mr. Churchill saw to it that the Fleet was not dispersed. On August 1, in defiance of the Cabinet's veto, he ordered that the Naval Reserve be mobilized and a few minutes after war was declared against Germany, the Fleet was on its way to engage the enemy.

"There is one thing they cannot take away from you," Lord Kitchener said to Mr. Churchill after the Gallipoli fiasco had forced him from the Admiralty. "The Fleet was ready!"

Gallipoli was the greatest tragedy of Mr. Churchill's life. It was a characteristically Churchillian plan of strategy—unorthodox and daring. Had it succeeded, the British would have secured an entry to the "back-door" of Europe. But Mr. Churchill underestimated the strength of the Turks and the opposition of the politicians and brass hats at home. By the middle of May 1915, it was obvious that the Gallipoli venture was doomed. In the Cabinet shake-up that took place at this time Mr. Churchill was ousted from the Admiralty into the Chancellorship of the Dutchy of Lancaster, a sinecure that carried with it a salary of $20,000 a year. He was excluded from the War Council and allowed no hand in the conduct of the war.

Three months earlier he had taken a seemingly

trivial decision that was to have momentous consequences. The Committee of Imperial Defense
had turned over to the Admiralty the blueprints
for a "landship" that would batter through the
enemy lines like a steamroller. Churchill was
enthusiastic and without Cabinet authorization
ordered eighteen of these monsters at a cost of
$350,000. This step had a curious sequel. When
Mr. Balfour took over the Admiralty, he can-
celled the order for all except one of the "land-
ships." A tryout of the lone survivor, nick-named
"Big Willie," impressed the War Office and in
February 1916 more of these machines were ordered. Production was started immediately under
the greatest secrecy. Tanks were used for the first
time at the Battle of Thiepval on September 15,
1916, and the result was sensational.

This time Churchill had been right, far too
right, alas, in the long count. He was destined to
witness in May and June of 1940 new and more
formidable versions of the monsters he had helped
bring into the battlefields sweeping over the Low
Countries, smashing through France's lines of defense, crashing their way irresistibly toward the

Channel ports until they came to a halt beside the sea, facing the white cliffs of Dover.

Mr. Churchill's tenure of the Dutchy of Lancaster was short-lived. The enforced idleness maddened him; he yearned to be up and doing. What was there for him to do? Why fight, of course. He was a soldier, and a good one. His decision gave him a new lease on life. He promptly applied for a commission and received a colonelcy in the Royal Scots Fusilliers.

Mr. Churchill's first act at the front was to obtain permission to be quartered in the trenches with his men instead of at battalion headquarters. This seemingly democratic gesture instantly established his popularity. His motives, he later confessed gaily, were the reverse of praiseworthy. The simple truth was that in the trenches you got a liquor ration whereas strict teetotalling was the rule in the officers' mess.

Even as a Colonel he showed little respect for official mumbo-jumbo. He shocked his fellow officers by wearing an exceptionally long trench coat surmounted by a riding stock and a blue French helmet instead of the regulation Glengarry bonnet. And on one occasion he greatly embarrassed two visiting generals by tactlessly showing them over a forward sector of his command that was being heavily shelled at the time.

"But this is very dangerous," said one of the big-wigs anxiously.

"Yes, indeed, sir," Mr. Churchill replied ironically. "This is a very dangerous war."

His most memorable act at the front was a lecture on lice which began, "Gentlemen, war is declared—on lice!" There followed a detailed and most scientific plan of campaign for the extermination of these pests. It was not long before Churchill's battalion was known on the Western Front as "the louseless battalion."

When Mr. Churchill resigned from the army, he left behind him a reputation for utter fearlessness. He seemed to his fellow soldiers completely oblivious to the constant threat of sudden death. No, not completely oblivious. There was a glint in his eye, a suspicion of repressed excitement about his manner that showed he was aware of the danger—and revelled in it! "Don't you love war?" he asked his men one night in the trenches. They were quite sure that for his part Colonel Churchill did.

This was the end of Mr. Churchill's soldiering. He had commanded troops on active service in Asia, Africa and Europe. He left the army with only one disappointment. He had been refused the post of general.

In July 1917, Mr. Churchill was restored to the Cabinet—thanks to the insistence of Lloyd George, then Prime Minister, who, like Churchill today, was determined to rally around him the best brains in the country. Mr. Churchill was placed in charge of the Ministry of Munitions which, in a few short weeks he revitalized and reorganized completely. But this was only the prelude of a far greater task. America had entered the war. Millions of American troops were waiting to take the field—as soon as they had the equipment. It was Mr. Churchill's job to provide it, most of it at any rate. It was a task after his own heart.

Mr. Churchill accepted from the head of the American War Industries Board—Mr. Bernard Baruch—a contract for $500,000,000 to supply the American Army with medium artillery. The two made a "gentleman's agreement" that the transaction would be conducted without profit or loss to either side. The scheme worked admirably, and it incidentally laid the foundation of one of the closest friendships of Mr. Churchill's life.

Mr. Churchill was in the Hotel Metropole in London, the headquarters of the Ministry of Munitions, when the news of the Armistice was brought to him. He showed no sign of jubilation. The time was past for rejoicing. England had been saved, yes, but it was no longer quite the same England; and Mr. Churchill was deeply conscious of the loss. Some years later he wrote somberly, "Scarcely anything which I was taught to believe permanent had lasted. Everything I was taught to believe impossible had happened." But the lesson was not lost on him. In 1932, when the war that in 1918 seemed unthinkable emerged as a distinct probability, Mr. Churchill's was the first voice raised in warning: "Fears in Europe are greater, rivalries are sharper, military organizations more carefully and efficiently developed and Britain is weaker. Britain's period of weakness is Europe's danger . . ."

After the Armistice Mr. Churchill received two offices, the War Office and the Air Ministry. He held these for three years and then became Colonial Secretary, in which capacity he was responsible for working out a settlement to the tangled problems of the Middle East.

The appearance of the First Labor Government in 1923 put him out of office; it also made him realize that his allegiance naturally belonged to the Conservative Party. Again the decision was uncannily well-timed. The Liberal Party was dead, though no one knew it then. The Conservatives at first by themselves, later by a shrewd compromise with Labor, have dominated English politics ever since.

For five years—from 1924 to 1929—Mr. Churchill was Chancellor of the Exchequer, as his father had been before him. His tenure of that office was, strangely enough, fairly uneventful. Though he held it for five years it was not a position he enjoyed. When Labor won the elections of 1929 and Mr. Churchill found himself out of office, he experienced at first a sensation of relief. There were so many books to be written, so many landscapes he wished to paint. On the proceeds of his *The World Crisis* he had bought himself a beautiful manor house in Kent. He dearly loved to don old blue overalls and construct miniature rock gardens in its grounds. At the moment, he did not understand the men of Westminster and they did not understand him. England would soon tire of these mediocrities and then his turn would come. In the meanwhile the role of country squire was not without charm.

Mr. Churchill was quick to realize his mistake. It was no temporary fit of apathy but a paralysis, a total blindness that had descended upon England. The Nazis were rapidly rearming Germany and England grew weaker day by day. He had found a new mission, the thankless role of a Tory Cassandra, and he threw himself into the fray. There was only one thing he could do and that was to warn his countrymen of their folly. For seven years he did it, without flagging or failing, while first Baldwin and then Chamberlain led England nearer to the brink of utter ruin.

There is a tragic irony in the fact that only when Mr. Churchill's prophesies of disaster had been proved true was he called upon to lend his wisdom, his intellectual brilliance and the force of his personality to the counsels of His Majesty's Government.

"They" put him in the Admiralty, those who

had for ten years kept him in the wilderness because he was "too clever," and the word was flashed to all ships "Winnie is back." The Navy knew he was their man and the people of England were beginning to realize it too. Insistent voices were clamoring for a real leader, a man who would stand up to Hitler and Mussolini, who would shake England out of the torpor that had beset her, who would inspire her men with confidence and courage and the determination to wipe out the evil thing that faced them, no matter what the cost. There was obviously only one such man in England—Winston Churchill. As the German Army launched its great offensive in the West, England finally turned to him to see her through the storm.

It was a grave, a solemn responsibility, but one he did not hesitate to accept. From his predecessors he took over a sinking ship without one word of recrimination: "If we wrangle about yesterday we have lost tomorrow," was his only reference to the days when Chamberlain's England slept.

He rallied a nation and lead it back to battle with renewed vigor when all of its allies were gone and its hope was a feeble flicker of light on a black horizon. He stemmed—at least for a while —the victorious onrush of the dictators and smashed the armies of Fascism in Africa. He kindled in the hearts of his countrymen a light that will burn brightly in the pages of England's history when the heartbreak and the tragedy of this war have become a dim memory.

England's finest hour belongs to Winston Churchill.

## ACKNOWLEDGMENT

Always, after the writing of a volume such as this, there are just debts happily to be paid by the author.

I want to say a warm "thank you" to Mr. William L. Chenery, editor of *Collier's Weekly;* to Mr. Charles Scribner and to Otto Pickhardt, M.D., one time personal physician to Winston Churchill, for their valuable help. I must also express especial appreciation to Mr. Charles Rolo for his invaluable assistance, for his patient advice and for his expert and painstaking criticism of my manuscript.